The Complete Guide to Pla

Book 2: Melodic Phr

Published by **www.fundamental-changes.com**

ISBN: 978-1495938450

Copyright © 2014 Joseph Alexander

The moral right of this author has been asserted.

All rights reserved. No part of this publication may be reproduced, stored in a retrieval system, or transmitted in any form or by any means, without the prior permission in writing of the publisher. The publisher is not responsible for websites (or their content) that are not owned by the publisher.

Fundamental Changes Ltd.

Also By Joseph Alexander

The Complete Guide to Playing Blues Guitar Book One: Rhythm Guitar

The Complete Guide to Playing Blues Guitar Book Three: Beyond Pentatonics

The Complete Guide to playing Blues Guitar Compilation

The CAGED System and 100 Licks for Blues Guitar

Fundamental Changes in Jazz Guitar: The Major ii V I

Minor ii V Mastery for Jazz Guitar

Jazz Blues Soloing for Guitar

Guitar Scales in Context

Guitar Chords in Context Part One

Jazz Guitar Chord Mastery (Guitar Chords in Context Part Two)

Complete Technique for Modern Guitar

The Complete Technique, Theory and Scales Compilation for Guitar

Sight Reading Mastery for Guitar

Rock Guitar Un-CAGED: The CAGED System and 100 Licks for Rock Guitar

The Practical Guide to Modern Music Theory for Guitarists

Beginner's Guitar: The Essential Guide

All audio downloads in this book are available from **www.fundamental-changes.com/audio-downloads**

Contents

Introduction 4

Chapter 1: Blues Guitar Soloing Basics 6

The Minor Pentatonic Scale 6
Simple Minor Pentatonic Blues Guitar Licks 9
Introducing Bends 10
Using Bends in Blues Licks 14
Sliding in and out of Blues Licks 15
Vibrato 18

Chapter 2: Rhythmic Divisions 21

1/8th notes in 12/8 21
1/16th notes in 12/8 22
Creating Melodies by Using Rhythmic Structures 25
Further Rhythms 30
Building Longer Lines 32
Silence 34
Duplets (2 against 3 feel) 40

Chapter 3: Rhythmic Displacement 44

Displacement on the Beat 44
Displacement by 1/8th Note Divisions of the Beat 48
Displacement by 1/16th Note Divisions of the Beat 52

Chapter 4: Developing Lines and Creativity 59

Creativity with Question and Answer Structures 59
Creativity by Limiting Rhythm 62
Creativity by Limiting Range 65
    Rhythm 65
    Beginning and Ending Notes 65
    Bending 66
    Duration/Frequency 66
    Pick Angle 67
    Articulation 67
Asking the Question 68

Developing a Melodic Line 72
Tonal Variation with Phrasing 75

Chapter 5: Range and Other Positions on the Neck 79

A Minor Pentatonic Shape Two 80
A Minor Pentatonic Shape Three 84
A Minor Pentatonic Shape Four 87
A Minor Pentatonic Shape Five 90
Linking Minor Pentatonic Shapes 93

Conclusions 94

Appendix A Bending in Tune 95

Bending 95
    Pre-bends 97
    Unison Bends 97
    Double Stop Bends 99

Appendix B Vibrato 100

    Axial Vibrato 100
    Radial Vibrato 101

Other Books from Fundamental Changes 104

Be Social 104

Introduction

The second book in this series on blues guitar playing focuses on the most important ideas, musical concepts and techniques that you will need to develop in order to become a well-rounded, competent and *expressive* blues guitar soloist.

This book is not simply a list of *The Hundred Greatest Blues Licks* or yet another *Play in the Style of...*

While I don't discount the usefulness of titles like these, what I am aiming to do in this book is to get deeper into the concepts of rhythm, phrasing, feel and melody that will take you to a new level in your playing.

The idea is to not simply teach you to play and regurgitate blues licks: I want to teach you to be in control of every note that you play. The goal is not to play 100 different blues licks; it is to be able to play 1 blues lick in 100 different ways.

If you listen to your favourite players *really* carefully, you will begin to notice similar 'parent' licks re-occurring throughout their solos. The reason that this is not immediately obvious is that these players are masters of manipulating their phrasing, rhythm and feel.

By thinking about your guitar solos in terms of rhythm and phrasing you will never run out of melodic ideas. You will never have to worry about forgetting your lines or being able to execute them live on stage. Your musical connection with your guitar will deepen and you will quickly develop the ability to express yourself through your guitar, rather than the all too common scenario of having to 'chase licks' around the fretboard.

When I introduce my private students to the concepts contained in this book, there is often a major paradigm shift. They will tend to start to think about music in terms of 'note placement' rather than the specific notes themselves. Of course, melody and note choice *is* important, but when you consider we all have the *same* 12 notes available to us, the only logical conclusion is that it is rhythm, phrasing, dynamics and articulation that set us apart from other players.

This is even truer in a blues guitar solo where we may only be playing 5 or 6 different pitches. It's very much a case of *when* you play, not *what* you play.

If you are looking for a book full of blues licks, don't despair! The first part of this book focuses on some of the important blues guitar basics, helping to get you into the sound of each important scale we use in the blues. In fact there are over 100 unique blues licks contained in these pages spread over the 5 most commonly used shapes for each scale we cover. It's important to get the sound of the language into your head before you start experimenting with the rhythm and phrasing concepts outlined later in the book.

If you need more blues guitar licks, my book The CAGED System and 100 Licks for Blues Guitar will teach you a complete system to learn the guitar while giving you 100 blues licks to get your teeth into.

What I hope to achieve with this book is a guide that is suitable for beginners but also for the intermediate and advancing guitarist: I use a system that is based on a more rhythmic, musical approach to improvisation rather than a simple copy-these-licks based one.

If you've been playing a while you may wish to skip some of the introductions to scales and jump to some of the more appropriate rhythm and phrasing sections. However, I would suggest that you do read the parts that you feel you might already know. There might be a little lick, trick or even a whole mental system that could make a subtle or intrinsic difference to your playing.

As always in my books, every notated example is available as a free download from **www.fundamental-changes.com/audio-downloads**. Thank you to my teacher Pete Sklaroff for recording them so musically and professionally.

I hope this book makes a positive difference to your playing. Some of the rhythmic exercises may be tricky at first but listen to the audio examples carefully and you'll get there. These days, rhythm and phrasing are about 70% of my practice time and I wish I'd known about the ideas in this book a long time ago.

For a more complete introduction to the roots of the blues, check out book one of this series, The Complete Guide to Blues Guitar Book One: Rhythm, where I give much more background on the roots of the blues and some essential listening.

Another reason that I recommend having a copy of book one in your possession is that book two does not give a huge amount of detail about the chords for the blues progressions that we are soloing *over*. The structure of the 12 bar blues is assumed knowledge and covered in meticulous detail in book one.

If you know how a 12 bar blues functions then you will get great insight into the building blocks of blues guitar soloing from this book. If not, then I suggest getting yourself familiar with this essential chord form either via The Complete Guide to Blues Guitar: Book One or via the multitude of free learning resources on the internet.

As always, have fun!

Joseph Alexander

All audio downloads in this book are available from

www.fundamental-changes.com/audio-downloads

Chapter 1: Blues Guitar Soloing Basics

The melodic language of blues originates from the 'spirituals', 'work songs' and 'field hollers' sung by African-Americans in the era of captivity, and in the years that followed emancipation. As a result, the blues is rich in African-American rhythm, harmony, melody and phrasing. One of the most important melodic structures that retains a strong link to this time is the performance of 'call and response', or antiphony, where one musical 'question' is sung, and is then answered by different voices.

When musicologists 'formalised' and incorporated the melodies they had transcribed into traditional western musical thinking (classical theory), they found that many of the melodies were formed from just 5 notes. The term 'pentatonic' refers to a scale that uses 5 notes to divide up the octave.

Pent = five,
Tonic = tones.

In addition to this *minor* pentatonic scale, they noticed that singers also often used their voices to slide and bend from one note smoothly into another. If you're reading on an eReader check out this incredible, short clip of an **early gospel choir**: if not, search for "Early African American Spiritual Gospel Choir", uploaded by *Patterickcoati*.

This music *may* be from a different age, but hearing the roots of the blues sound helps us to understand the language of the music that we play today. This is why our scale choice, use of bending, vibrato and slides are so important: these sounds are the essence of the blues and form the basis of virtually all modern music.

The Minor Pentatonic Scale

We will begin by breaking down the language of the blues into a simple alphabet: the minor pentatonic scale. In the key of A, we can play the minor pentatonic scale as follows:

Example 1a:

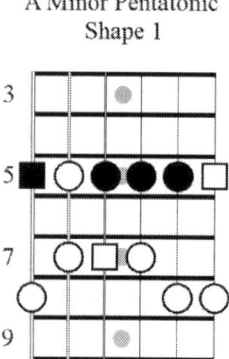

A MINOR PENTATONIC SHAPE 1

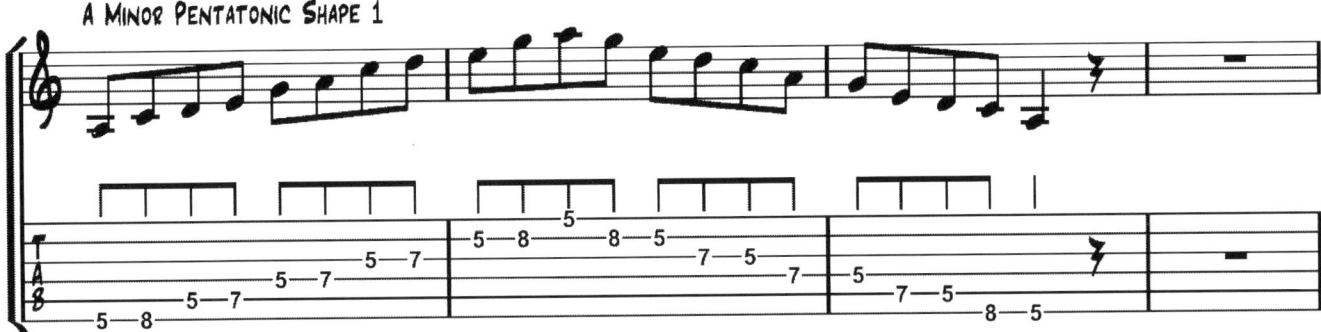

The coloured or dark notes in the scale diagram form a minor 7 chord. It is a good idea to learn a chord shape in conjunction with every scale shape to aid your memory. Throughout this book, every scale shape will have a chord shown within it. Think of it as a chord 'anchor' to help you organise your thinking. For more details of how to use chords to break up the fretboard check out my book, the CAGED System and 100 Licks for Blues Guitar.

This first shape (there are five to eventually learn) of the minor pentatonic scale is one of the most common scale shapes used by guitarists. It is the melodic starting point for thousands of guitarists learning to solo and you may already be familiar with it. We will of course progress beyond this shape and access other areas of the guitar neck but for now learn its pattern thoroughly.

Begin by playing this scale shape ascending and descending and try out these melodic patterns to get the sound of the scale into your ears.

Example 1b:

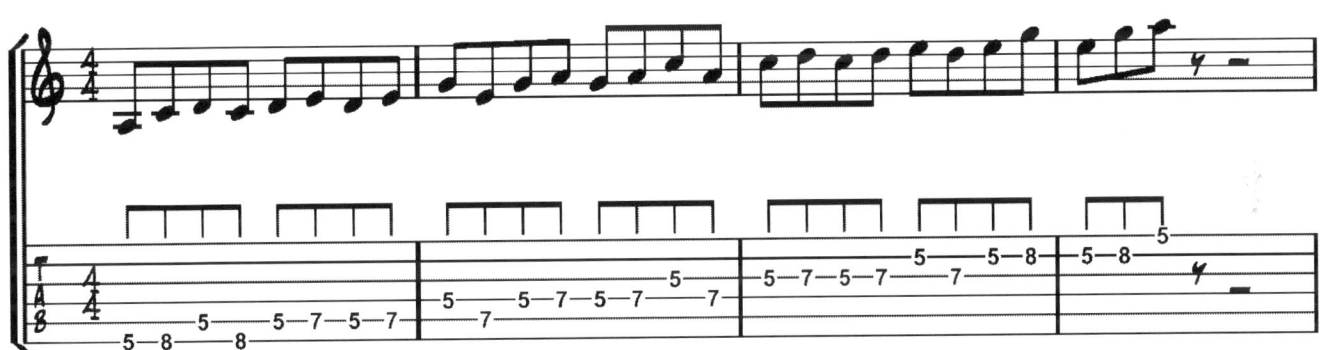

Example 1c:

Play through these patterns both forwards and backwards.

Just as learning a new alphabet does not automatically allow us to speak a foreign language, you may well be struggling to hear 'the blues' in the previous examples. We are, after all, simply playing some scale patterns. What we need are some actual phrases and an idea of the *structure* of the language to help us learn how it functions.

The first thing to note is that the previous two examples were both written in 4/4 time. As you know from book one, the notes in 4/4 tend to divide *evenly* into groups of two and four. We will discuss rhythm in *much* greater detail later, but for now it is enough to say that most blues isn't played with an even feel.

The majority of blues that you will hear is played in *triplet* time.

In other words, throughout this piece of music we can count:

1 2 3 1 2 3 1 2 3 1 2 3

This is known as 12/8 time as there are 12, 1/8th notes in each bar. Each of the four beats is grouped into three 1/8th notes.

Playing the pentatonic scale with this triplet feel automatically sounds a little bit bluesier. You can hear this when you play **example 1d:**

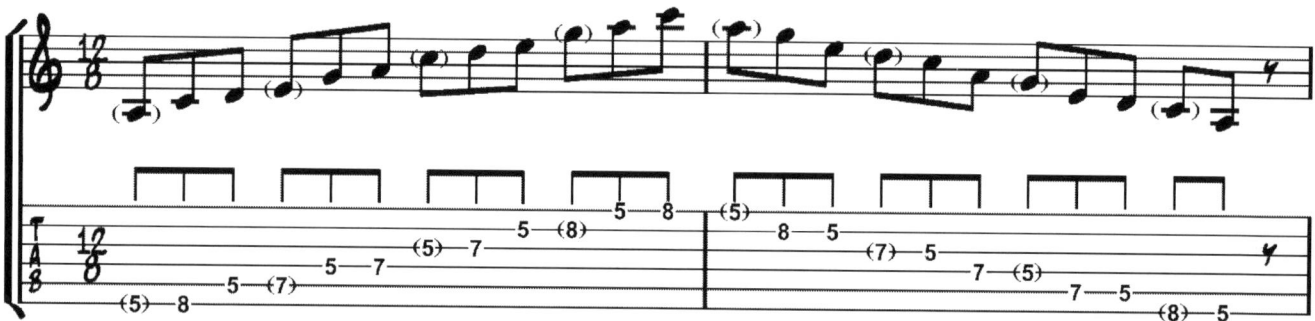

Try to give a slight accent to the first of each group of three notes (shown in brackets).

Try playing the minor pentatonic scale with this triplet feel over backing track one. Hopefully you will begin to hear your playing become a little bit bluesier.

Simple Minor Pentatonic Blues Guitar Licks

Playing a scale straight up and down in this way is little more than reciting an alphabet. We can arrange these *letters* into short *words* and *phrases* which begin to make sense to the listener. Play through the following examples and try them with backing track one when you feel confident.

Example 1e:

Example 1f:

Example 1g:

These first few examples contain nothing in the way of phrasing marks, bends, slides or any of the other subtleties that we use to make the music vocal and alive. They are simply some strong melodic lines that start to get us into the ballpark of the blues language and by playing them you will start to train your ears and fingers to find melodic shapes on the fretboard.

Introducing Bends

Now we will look at how we can bend notes to mimic the sound of a blues vocalist. Blues bends are one of the most important techniques we can use to sound authentic on the guitar.

You may remember from book one that the chords played in the rhythm guitar part of a blues are normally dominant 7. These chords are a special kind of major-type chord and contain a *major 3rd* which defines the major or 'happy' sound. The scale that we have been using to create our melodic lines is the *minor* pentatonic scale. It contains a b3 (flat three) interval which defines its minor or 'sad' sound. This can be seen clearly on the guitar when you view a dominant 7 chord next to the minor pentatonic scale.

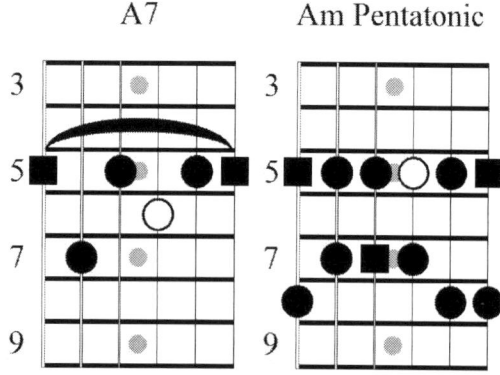

Look at the note on the 3rd string, 6th fret in the A7 diagram. Notice that this is different from the note in the A minor pentatonic scale on the 3rd string *5th* fret. These two notes, a semitone apart (C# and C) will tend to clash and many classical musicians would say this is undesirable. It certainly isn't the greatest sound if you just 'sit' on the minor 3rd and don't manipulate the note in any way. You can hear a b3 against the major 3rd in **example 1h:**

I hope you can hear that this isn't the greatest sound in the world!

The answer to this problem is to give the minor 3rd (C) a little bend up towards the major 3rd (C#).

To achieve this, use your 1st finger to bend the string towards the floor slightly raising its pitch. I will normally put my thumb on the top of the fretboard to provide strength, leverage and support.

10

While this isn't a technique book I have included some useful bending intonation exercises in appendix A.

When we add bends to the previous exercise we may catch a glimpse of the blues guitar sound. Don't worry too much if you don't have the strength with your first finger to bend all the way to C#. Often when we bend this note we won't push the C all the way to C# anyway. A lot of fun can be had seeing how many different microtones we can find between the b3 and major 3.

Listen carefully to **exercise 1i** which demonstrates the minor 3rd being bent all the way up to the major 3rd.

Example 1i:

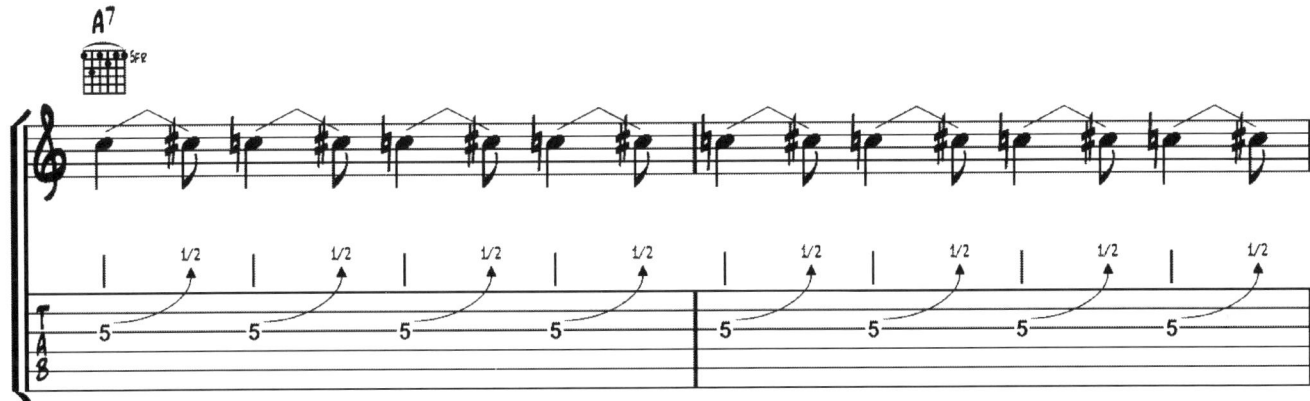

Now compare example 1i with **example 1j** where we don't necessarily make it all the way to C#.

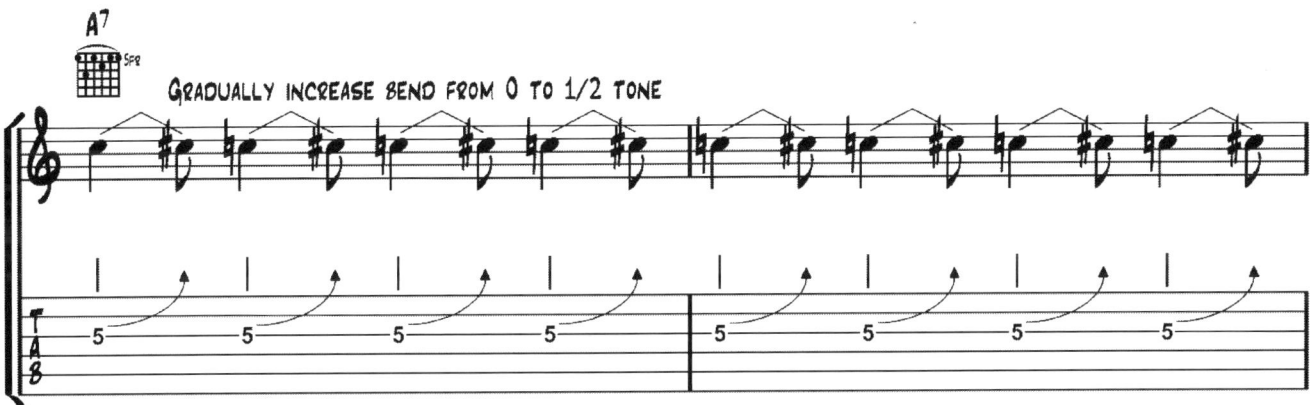

As I mentioned, we will talk much more about the subtleties of this kind of nuance in a later chapter but for now it is good to be aware that we can just give the minor 3rd a little nudge towards major 3rd territory. When we slightly bend a note in this way it is often called a *curl*.

Now let's look at other common bends that occur in blues guitar before incorporating them into some useful blues licks.

We can bend from the 4th of the A minor pentatonic scale (D) to either the b5 (Eb) or the natural 5 (E).

The 'b5' note (Eb) is often called the 'blues note' as it is extremely common in the blues sound. In fact there is a scale called 'the blues scale' which we will learn later. The blues scale is simply the minor pentatonic scale with the addition of the b5 note.

Begin by practicing the bend from the 4th to the b5th (semitone bend) and then bending from the 4th to the natural 5th (whole tone bend).

Use your 3rd finger to bend the D note and support the 3rd finger with your 1st and 2nd fingers added on the string behind it for extra strength. Try to get it absolutely in tune with the recorded audio examples.

Example 1k (a and b):

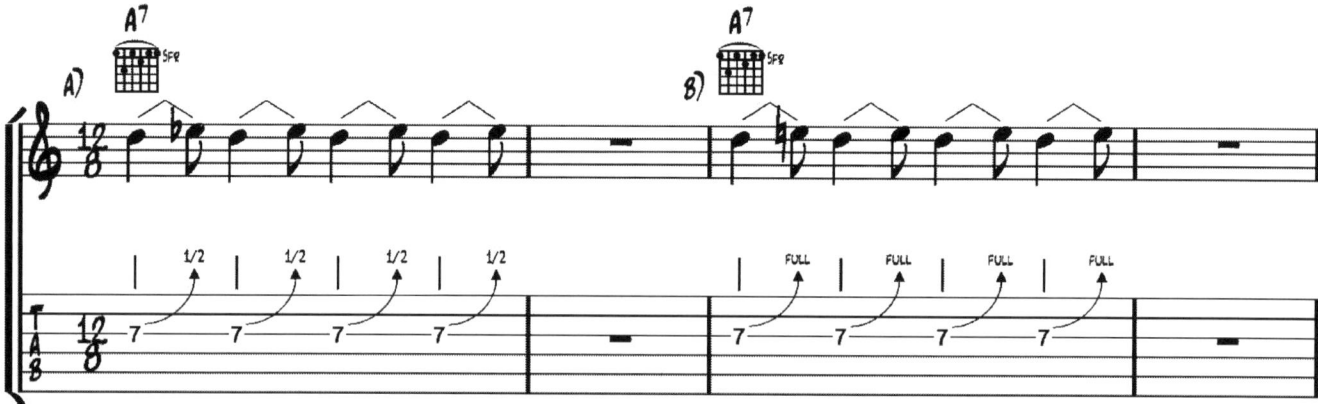

Finally, another common bend is from the b7 (G) to the root (A). Practice playing this bend with your 3rd finger and then your 4th finger. Again, support the bend by placing your spare fingers on the string behind the bent note. This will help with strength, accuracy and control.

Example 1l:

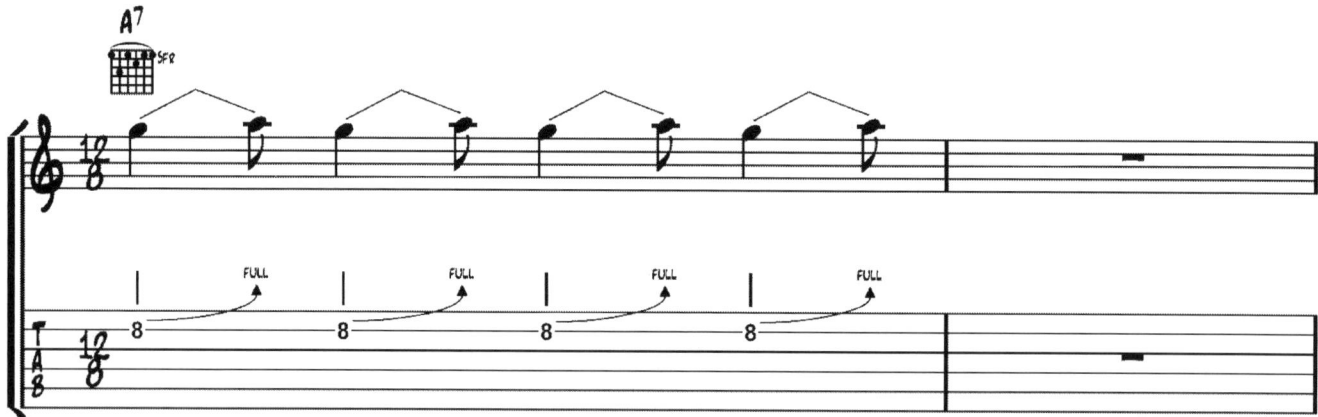

With the bend from the b7 to the root it is essential that you work hard to develop your accuracy. The root of the scale is such a strong note and an inaccurate bend here will sound terrible.

To help you increase your accuracy, practice the exercises in appendix A on page 96.

There are other places in this scale where bends are effective. Experiment by working through the scale and try to bend each note in turn.

Now we have studied some important bends in the minor pentatonic scale we will begin to incorporate them into useful blues guitar licks in the next section.

Using Bends in Blues Licks

The following minor pentatonic lines are rhythmically simple and incorporate bent notes into them. Remember to *always* support the bent note with any spare fingers and listen carefully to make sure your bend is in tune.

There are many different ways to phrase a bend; slow, fast, immediate, delayed or gradual. We will discuss these ideas when we get into *phrasing* in chapter three. For now, do your best to exactly match the phrasing on the audio track.

Examples 1m - 1p:

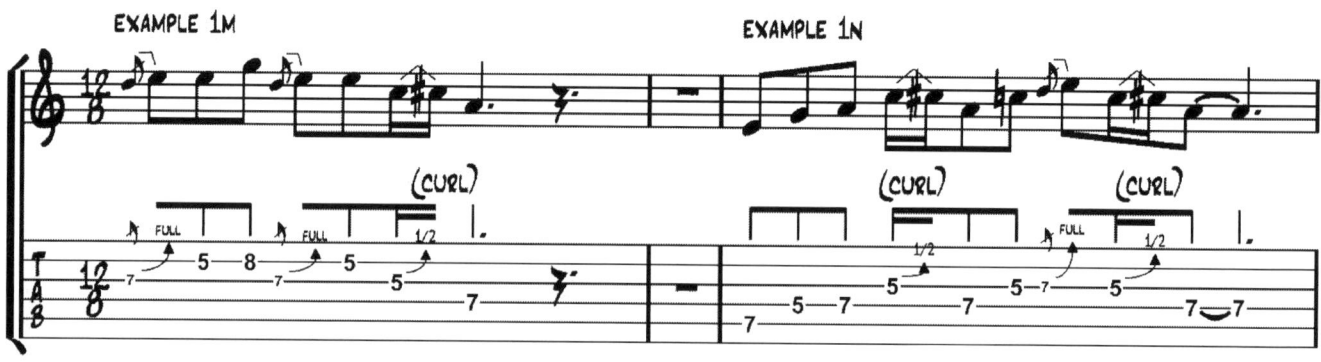

Remember to keep a strict '1 2 3 1 2 3' feel to these lines at first. Learn them by syncing your playing to the recorded audio examples before playing them against backing track one. Once you have learnt them thoroughly don't worry about sticking to the exact timings written here; make them your own by varying the rhythms and phrase lengths. Chapter three will give you many ideas about how you can begin to alter licks to suit your own personal taste and feel.

Hopefully you can see that by adding just these bends, the pentatonic scale comes alive with bluesy melodic possibilities. Bent notes are an intrinsic and vital part of the blues guitar (and vocal) sound and without them we're often left just playing scales.

Sliding in and out of Blues Licks

Continuing with the theme of mimicking a human voice, let's think for a minute about how our bodies create a vocal sound. Say the syllable 'huh' out loud. Pay careful attention to the way the first 'H' is formed in your throat and larynx. Can you hear and feel the 'breathy' noise in your throat before your vocal folds engage and the Huh noise 'catches' in your throat?

This little lead-in to a vocal sound can be replicated on a guitar by sliding into the first note of any phrase. A diagonal line before the start of a phrase shows that you should begin a phrase with a slide, however in practice it will rarely be notated as you will soon get into the habit of sliding into most of your melodic phrases.

Compare the following.

Examples 1q and 1r:

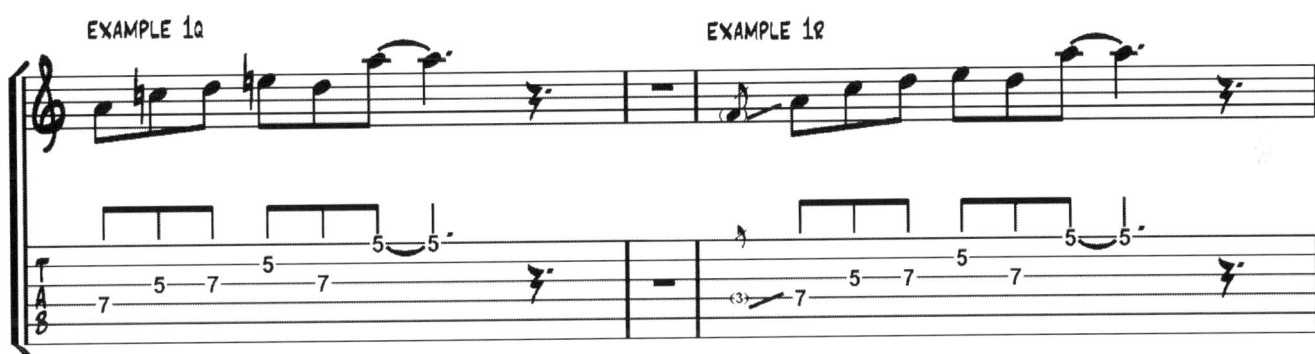

Example 1q is played 'flat' whereas example 1r is preceded by a grace-note slide into the first note of the phrase. Use your third finger to play this slide so you are in position to execute the rest of this lick.

Which line do you prefer the sound of? In my opinion, the second line has much more of a vocal quality to it and contains more energy and flow.

In example 1r I begin the slide from the 3rd fret however the starting point of the slide isn't that important. Try starting the slide from the 1st fret or the 6th fret. Try moving your finger slowly or quickly up the neck too. You can get some very interesting results simply by playing the slide in different ways. If you slide slowly, you will need to begin the movement slightly earlier so that you always hit the target note on the first beat of the bar.

If you're feeling brave, try adding a grace-note slide to the final note in the phrase. You'll have to be quick but this is a great way to emphasise the melodic leap in the melody.

It is equally possible to slide into a note from *above* in the same way.

Listen carefully to the next example where I slide into the D note at the start of the line. This is a little trickier technically but generates some great results. As before the priority should be making sure that the first note of the phrase falls in time on the first beat of the bar.

Example 1s:

Again, try sliding from different distances into the first note of the phrase.

Now let's combine a descending slide with an ascending slide using the previous example.

Example 1t:

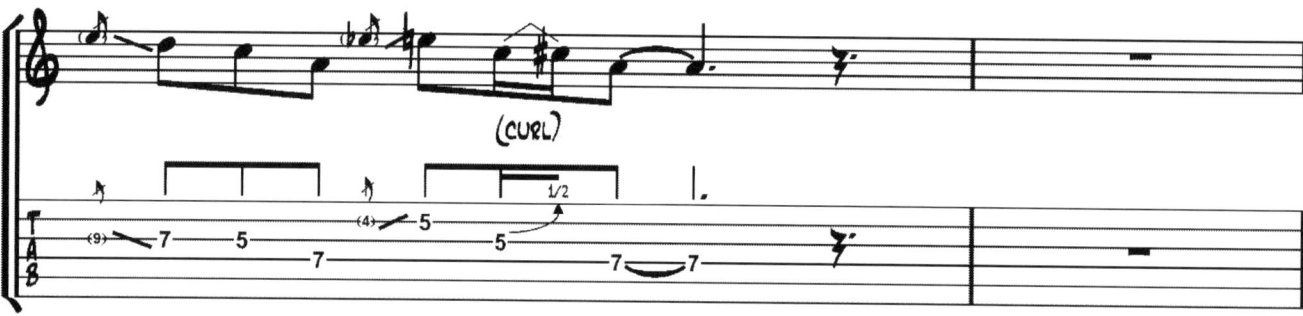

In example 1t, I slide into the second half of the phrase from a semitone below, hinting at the 'blues note' described earlier but you can slide from anywhere you like.

Often these kinds of slides are not notated as they are normally difficult to define musically, but you should get into the habit of using them often in your playing.

Let's return to the analogy of speaking for a moment.

Our voice does not die away the instant that our mouth closes. There is always going to be some kind of natural decay to our voice. Say 'Huh' out loud again and this time listen carefully to the end of the note. It can be difficult to hear but there will be a bit of natural reverberation (echo) to your voice as the sound bounces around the surfaces around you. As the sound gets absorbed by these surfaces it loses energy and gradually (or quickly) fades away.

If you're struggling to hear this, imagine that you are in a large, empty concert hall. How does your 'Huh' sound now? What about in a cave or a desert?

Good singers enhance this type of decay and add *vibrato* to their voices by controlling their diaphragms. If we are to learn to play with the vocal qualities of a singer it is important we learn to recreate this phenomenon on the guitar.

We can break this decay of sound down into two distinct areas; *Sliding out of phrases* and *vibrato*.

We shall start with the easier of the two areas - sliding out of phrases. This technique is unsurprisingly the exact opposite of sliding into notes that we just studied. We simply add a descending slide to the final note of the phrase.

Here is example 1t again, but this time with the added slide at the end.

Example 1u:

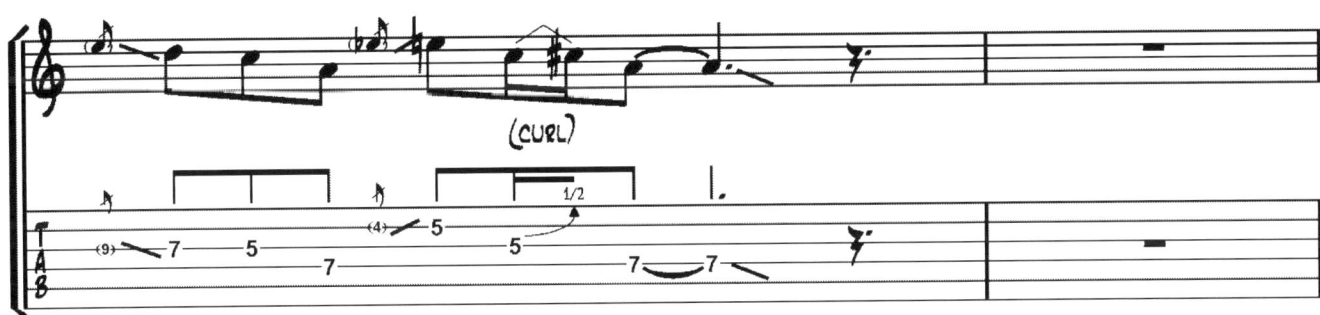

Notice that there is no indication of where you should finish this slide. I often end up around the 1st fret but there are no hard and fast rules here. To end the descending movement, practice releasing your finger pressure as you come to the end of the slide but don't let your finger lose contact with the guitar string when you stop. This will prevent the open string ringing which may be out of key with the song.

Once again, you have some interesting creative options here. How long are you going to let that final note ring for before you slide out of it? How quickly are you going to slide away from the note? - Too slowly and you may hear the individual frets sound as you move, too quickly and you risk sounding jerky and uncontrolled.

Try taking licks that you have learnt earlier and practice sliding in and out of them. Make up short phrases using the minor pentatonic scale and try to keep your fretting hand moving in a circular fashion as you slide in and out of each line. You can use big, small, fast and slow slides and add them in the middle of phrases either ascending *or* descending. Try to use subtlety and grace and then really overdo it by sliding into or out of *every* note. Don't worry about playing in time! With enough experimentation you will find a way to make these techniques your own and to develop your own unique voice when playing blues guitar.

Vibrato

Now we move on to the more difficult of the two techniques that we use to end a phrase; vibrato. Vibrato is a technique that most guitarists never stop practicing. It takes time to develop the strength, control, rhythm and subtlety it requires to play good vibrato so it is best to get started early in your soloing career.

Vibrato is essentially adding 'wobble' to the end of each phrase. It is an extremely vocal quality and in my opinion it can be one of the main factors that separate an 'OK' guitarist from a very good one.

To add vibrato to a note we move the string quickly up and down in a series of lots of fast bends. The further we bend the note the wider and more pronounced the vibrato will be.

Listen to **example 1v**, in part A the note C is held for two beats before a small and subtle vibrato is added to the end of the note. In part B, the note is again held for two beats but then a wider, more obvious vibrato is added.

Example 1v:

The technique for executing controlled vibrato can be fairly tricky so the exercises are included in appendix B on page 101. The basic idea is to try to play the vibrato with the *side* of the fingertip rather than the point.

By adding even narrow, subtle vibrato to the end of a phrase we can make the melody much more lyrical and flowing.

Here is example 1u again, but this time I have added soft vibrato to the end of the phrase.

Example 1w:

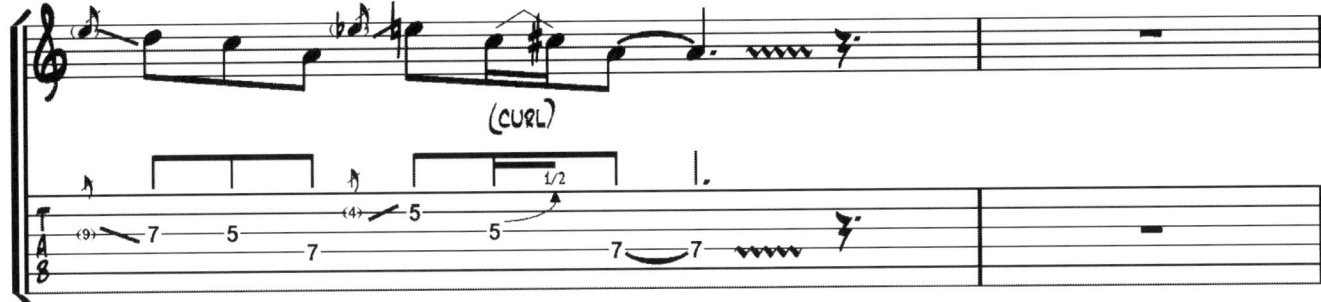

All we need to do now is add in the slide-off on the last note and the phrase is complete.

Example 1x:

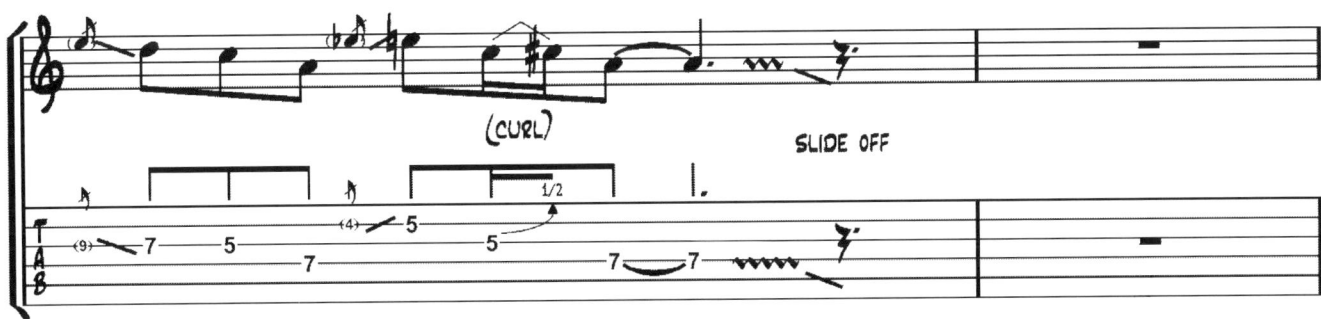

To give you some idea of how far we have come, listen first to the phrase above with no expressive techniques or bends and then listen to the phrase with all the articulations added. I hope you will agree that the difference is enormous. Try it yourself with backing track one. **Example 1y:**

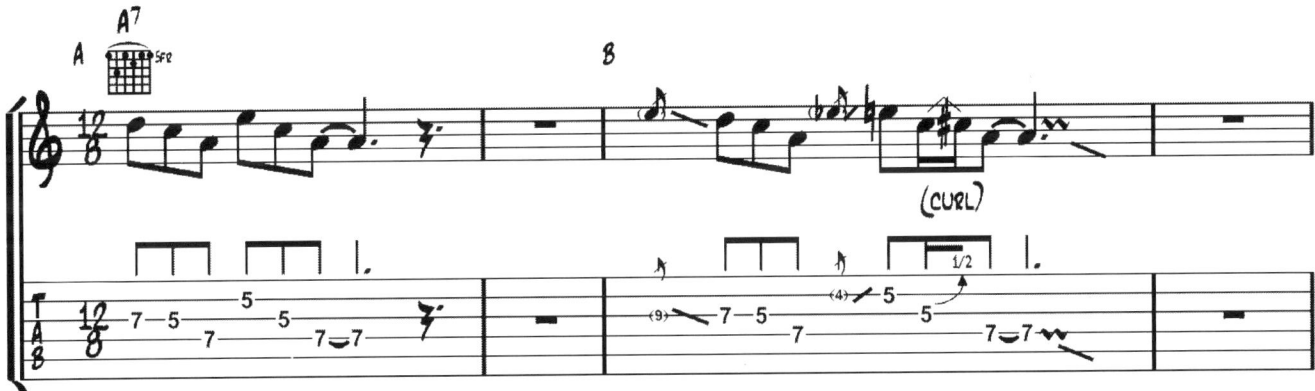

Sliding and vibrato aren't just for the beginnings and endings of phrases; you can, and should use them in the *middle* of blues licks too as shown in the following example.

Example 1z:

Listen very carefully to the audio example to pick up the nuances in this phrase. The starting points for the slides (in brackets) are only suggestions so use whatever distance feels right to make the line flow. Try this line out with the slow blues backing track and combine it with the other licks in this chapter to make a short solo.

Work through Appendix B in your own time to help develop the control of your vibrato and for more information check out my book **Complete Technique for Modern Guitar**

It may seem like I'm over emphasising the concept of articulation here, especially so early in the book but the truth is that these techniques and approaches to just a few notes *are* the difference between playing scales and playing music. Practice varying the slides (glissandos) and vibrato on every phrase that you learn. Make a point to experiment with these ideas as much as possible and you will *quickly* develop your own voice.

Chapter 2: Rhythmic Divisions

In the introduction to this book I spoke about how musicians all have access to the same 12 notes, but it is *how* and *when* we play them that set us apart from one another. If we don't want to be the kind of blues soloist who just regurgitates lick after lick, it is imperative that we learn to understand and control the rhythmic content of our playing.

When we can manipulate and alter our rhythmic phrasing at will, that is the point where we can stop learning the basics of the language and begin to tell our own story. In this chapter we will refresh the basic building blocks of rhythm and learn how we can use these building blocks to create structure in a solo and develop our *melodic* content.

1/8th notes in 12/8

So far in this book the examples and licks we have studied have all been fairly simple in terms of their rhythmic content. In this chapter we will learn how to subdivide these basic rhythms to generate an almost infinite amount of different blues phrases.

I mentioned on page 9 that the majority of blues tunes are written in the time signature of 12/8. Let's take a look at exactly what this means.

In as simple terms as possible 12/8 time tells us that there are *four beats in each bar* and each of the four beats is *divided into three subdivisions*. This can be seen in the following diagram.

Example 2a:

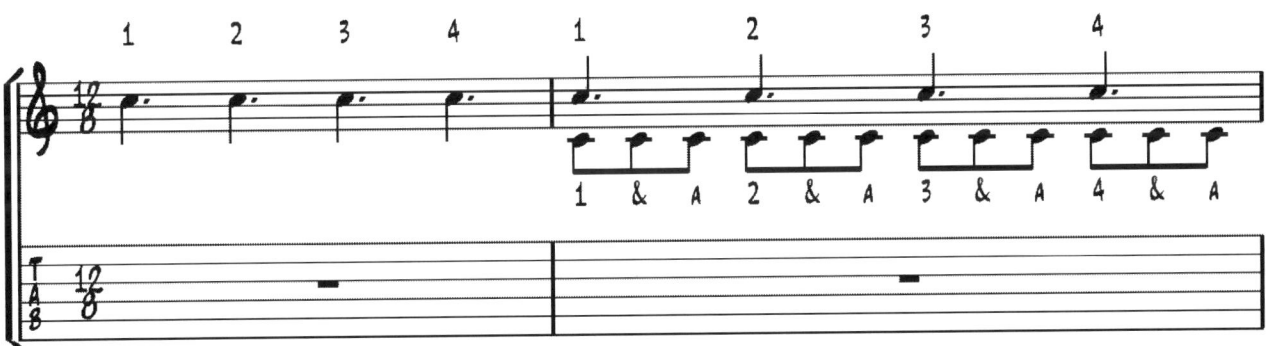

Listen to backing track one and count out loud "**one** and a **two** and a **three** and a **four** and a" throughout. Play an ascending A minor pentatonic scale in time with the track, and *accent* the first of each group of three notes. If you're not sure of how this feels, go back and listen to example 1d.

Because there are *three* 1/8th notes for every main beat of the bar, 12/8 is often referred to as a *triplet feel*. This is extremely important to understand because when we're soloing we normally want to 'lock in' with the rest of the band.

As each main beat of a 12/8 bar contains *three* 1/8th notes instead of the normal two you would see in 4/4, a single beat of music in 12/8 is written as a *dotted* 1/4 note. This is shown in the first bar of example 2a. To get a feel for this type of beat division, try this simple lick that combines 1/4 notes with 1/8th notes.

Example 2b:

Begin by only focusing on rhythmic accuracy but try to repeat the example adding in the slides, curls and vibrato that you learnt about in the previous chapter.

Most of the licks in chapter one used this kind of combination of 1/4 notes and 1/8th notes to create short phrases, but what happens if we want to 'change gears' and play a little faster?

1/16th notes in 12/8

To access a new, quicker rhythmic level we can split each 1/8th note into two and therefore double the amount of notes we are playing in each bar. We have now accessed the *1/16th note* rhythmic level.

This is shown in **example 2c:**

Notice that the *1st*, *3rd* and *5th* 1/16th notes in each beat line up perfectly with the 1/8th note above it.

Try ascending and descending the minor pentatonic scale using this subdivision as shown in the next example.

Example 2d:

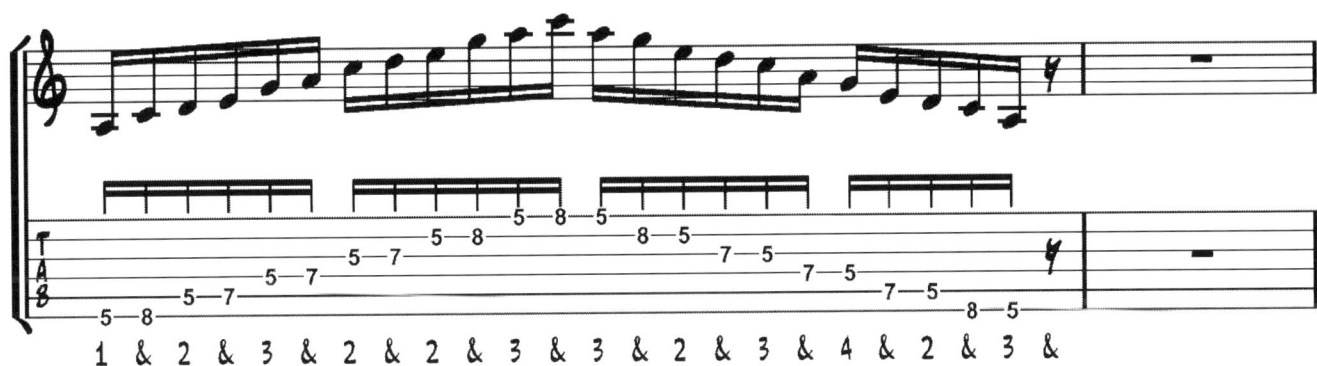

A very useful way to practice this kind of note division is to set your metronome to a very quick speed and to hear the click as the 1/8th note division. Using your metronome in this way means that every *three* clicks is one beat.

Set your metronome to 180 bpm (beats per minute). As the click is now playing the 1/8th notes this is the equivalent of the tempo being 60 bpm

With each click count out loud "**one** and a **two** and a **three** and a **four** and a" etc.

Now practice moving between one bar of 1/8th notes and switching to one bar of 1/16th notes against the metronome. Begin by repeating just one note but then move on to either playing the full pentatonic scale or short melodic phrases.

Example 2e:

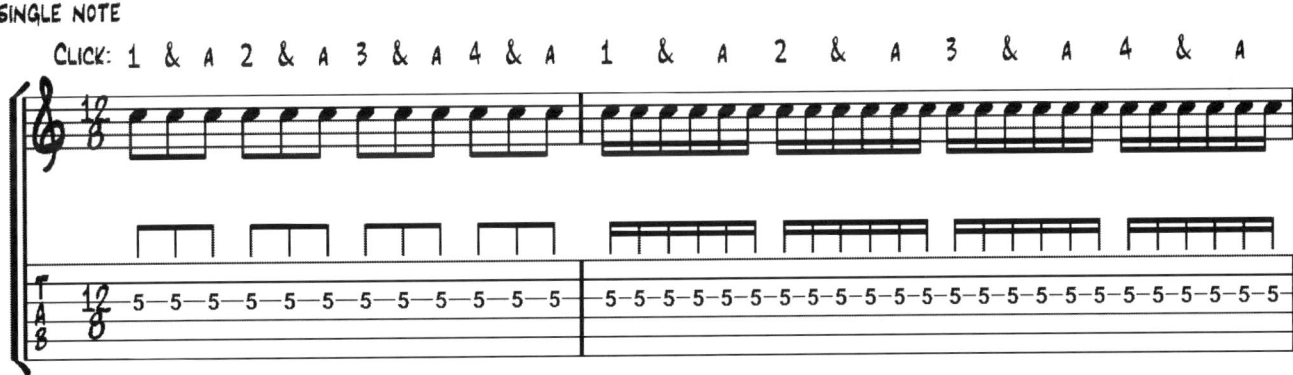

Example 2f:

In the previous example, don't worry too much about playing the notes exactly as written; the main challenge is switching between the 1/8ths and 1/16ths.

Finally, try changing between 1/8th and 1/16ths every beat.

Example 2g:

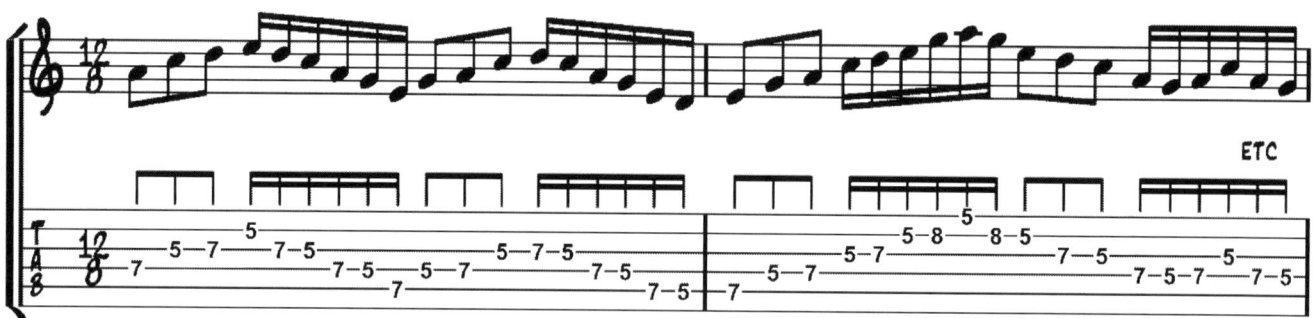

Once again, in example 2g don't worry about *which* notes you are playing, just make sure you are changing rhythmic divisions every beat. Let your fingers go for a walk around the pentatonic scale and get used to *changing gear* in this way.

If these divisions are too fast for you reduce the metronome speed to 150. Remember, the metronome is clicking the 1/8th notes, *not the beat* as you may be used to. The real tempo is three times slower than the metronome speed. 180 bpm = 60 bpm and 150 bpm = 50 bpm.

Creating Melodies by Using Rhythmic Structures

Although the previous few exercises may not have felt exceptionally 'bluesy' to you, the next few ideas will put these rhythmic exercises into musical context and show you that it is extremely simple to start constructing your own individual blues phrases.

Once you have the grasp of switching accurately between 1/8th notes and 1/16th notes, it is time to start combining these rhythmic subdivisions in the space of just one beat.

Look at and listen to the following rhythm:

Example 2h:

The first two divisions of beat one are 1/8th notes and the last division is two 1/16th notes. Notice that I finish the phrase with a one-beat note on beat two - this is to give the rhythm a sense of completion.

Put on backing track one and play the above rhythm for two full choruses. This may be a little harder than you imagine because it requires some degree of discipline not to meander off and start varying the rhythm of the phrase.

Next, try creating a few melodic phrases that stick *precisely* to this rhythm. Here are some examples:

Example 2i (a-d):

Notice that they all start on beat one of the bar, end on beat two and are identical to the rhythm shown above. Although these licks are designed to 'show you the way', the real goal is for you to use the A minor pentatonic scale to create *your own* lines that stick precisely to this rhythm.

In other words, when you have developed a *feel* for this rhythm by using the licks above, I want you to improvise a solo over backing track one using **only** the rhythm of the phrase, but altering the melody of the notes each time.

Use the A minor pentatonic scale as your source of melody, but *do not deviate from this rhythm*. This is actually a lot harder than you may think as the impulse to 'noodle' answering phrases in the gaps is normally quite powerful.

Begin your phrase on beat one of each bar and *do not play in the gaps!*

Example 2j is not notated here, but shows clearly what this kind of exercise should sound like.

The previous few examples were formed by doubling the note frequency on the 3rd division of the beat. i.e., we played two 1/16th notes instead of one 1/8th note.

We can play two 1/16th notes in place of *any* of the 1/8th notes in a beat. For example our rhythm could be the one shown in example 2k (a) which would give us phrases like examples 2k (b-d).

Don't forget to freely add in the slides and vibrato we discussed in chapter one to make these lines sound vocal and musical. **Example 2k (a-d):**

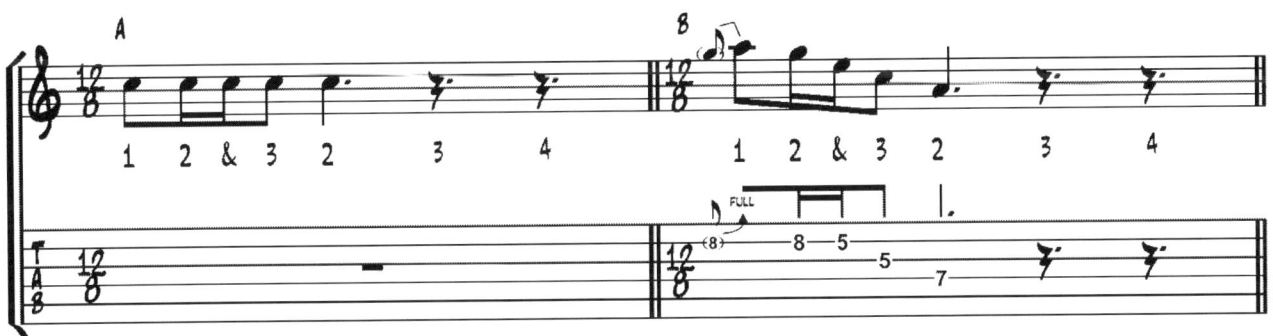

Once again, try improvising a 12 bar solo with the minor pentatonic scale but sticking rigidly to the rhythmic structure above.

When you're comfortable with the previous rhythm, try doubling the *first* division of the beat as shown in **example 2l (a-d)**. Then try improvising one more solo using this set rhythmic pattern.

Example 21 (a-d):

When you improvise your blues solos sticking to one of the rhythmic patterns given above, you should start to notice a great *strength* in your melodic lines.

Your ears will easily latch on to the structure of the rhythmic pattern and you will find that it hardly matters which notes from the pentatonic scale you use; everything you play will sound musically *linked* like lines from one big story.

These rhythmic ideas are obviously repetitive and we will be elaborating on this basic concept, but I hope you are starting to see the value of approaching your solos from a primarily rhythmic point of view - at least for a while.

We have looked at the following three rhythmic fragments:

and practiced using each one exclusively throughout a simple blues guitar solo.

Let's try taking each of the above structures in turn and using it to create short phrases *twice* in each bar.

Your solo may sound something like this next example but remember; this is just my improvisation, you can spend many hours coming up with new melodies with just one of these rhythmic fragments. Remember to use all the articulations from chapter one to colour the lines and help to make them melodic.

Example 2m:

Play full 12 bar solos with each of the rhythmic fragments in example 2l. Try strictly sticking to just one or just two occurrences of the phrase in each bar.

Now try *mixing* two rhythmic structures together. You can do this starting with one phrase per bar and then move on to two phrases per bar. For example,

Example 2n (a-b):

Can you hear that by combining rhythmic combinations in this way we start to develop the *call and response* phrasing that was mentioned at the beginning of chapter one?

Spend time in your practice session combining these three different rhythmic fragments and varying the frequency at which you play them. By doing this you will *internalise* the rhythms and they will become an unconscious part of your melodic improvisational approach.

Further Rhythms

So far, we have split just *one* of the three subdivisions of the beat into 1/16th notes. We can create many further permutations by splitting *two* of the divisions into 1/16ths. Here are the possibilities:

Example 2o:

We have covered rhythm D in example 2d so we will not look at it again here.

Here are two phrases to help you hear each of rhythms A, B and C:

Example 2p (a-f):

Once again, these melodic phrases are just here to help you to hear the rhythms in example 2o.

Practice taking *just one* of the rhythms and soloing *exclusively* with that rhythm over backing track one.

Stick to that rhythm and explore the minor pentatonic scale coming up with as many different melodies as you can. Begin by playing each rhythm just once in a bar, then twice in a bar.

When you feel you have exhausted all your possibilities,[1] try combining two of the rhythms from example 2o in the same way.
Finally, try to combine all three rhythms in your solo by first playing one phrase per bar and then by playing two phrases per bar.

---

[1] You haven't!

Building Longer Lines

Let's briefly recap all the rhythms we have covered so far in this chapter.

When we want to build longer melodic phrases we can simply combine two or more of these rhythms together.

The following process may look a bit 'academic' on paper, however if you take the time to isolate and build melodies from each of these rhythms in the previous 'further rhythms' section you should be able to jump straight in without having to spend too much time planning your licks in this way. Always let your melodic ear guide you.

Let's try combining rhythm F with rhythm B. To help us get a sense of resolution we will again end the phrase on a beat.

Example 2q (a-b):

How about combining rhythms C and G?

Example 2r:

Why not try rhythms H and C together?

Example 2s:

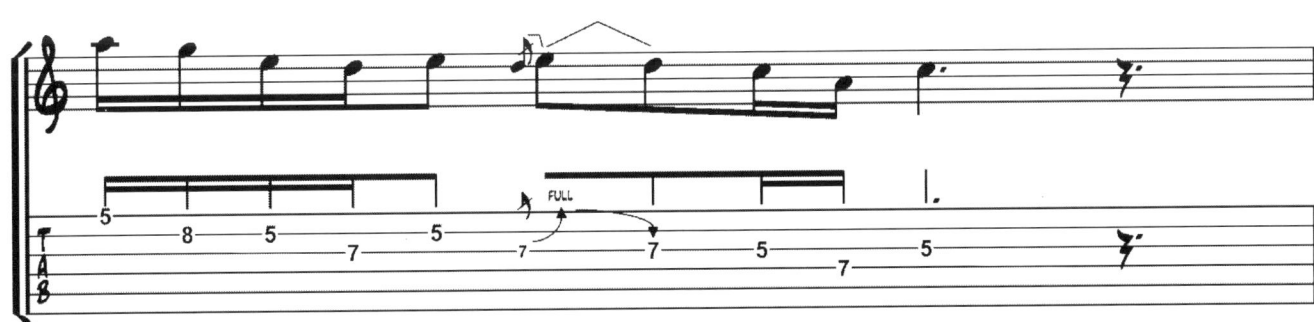

We have covered just nine common rhythms so far which gives us over 80 possibilities to combine them into unique rhythmic phrases. When you consider you can choose to play *any* note on *any* rhythmic division the melodic possibilities are almost infinite; especially when you realise you can make even longer phrases by just adding another rhythm.

The lesson to take away here is that many of the phrases you will hear and create are formed from just these nine basic, manageable rhythm 'chunks'. To speak a language unconsciously you must first start to hear and understand some of its fundamental building blocks - when these rhythms are all internalised into your melodic consciousness you won't even have to think about what you're playing anymore. Rhythm and pitch will naturally combine into strong, structured melodic solos.

Silence

We have discovered many possible permutations of rhythms that we can use to build interesting, unique phrases in our guitar solos, however, one extremely important factor we haven't considered yet is silence.

Using rests (beats of silence) lets us get really creative with our melodic phrasing by simply missing out a few notes.

Here are the main rest values that we need to be aware of when playing in 12/8.

The rests are written along the top with their corresponding note values written below.

Using example 2s as a 'workhorse' let's explore what happens when we insert these rests in turn into the first beat of the bar.

Example 2t (a - f):

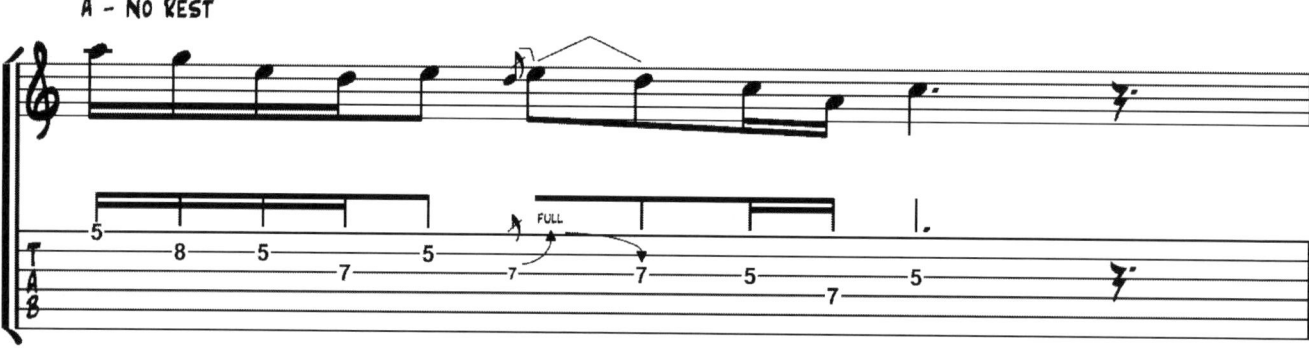

B - Whole Beat Rest

C - Two 1/8th note rests

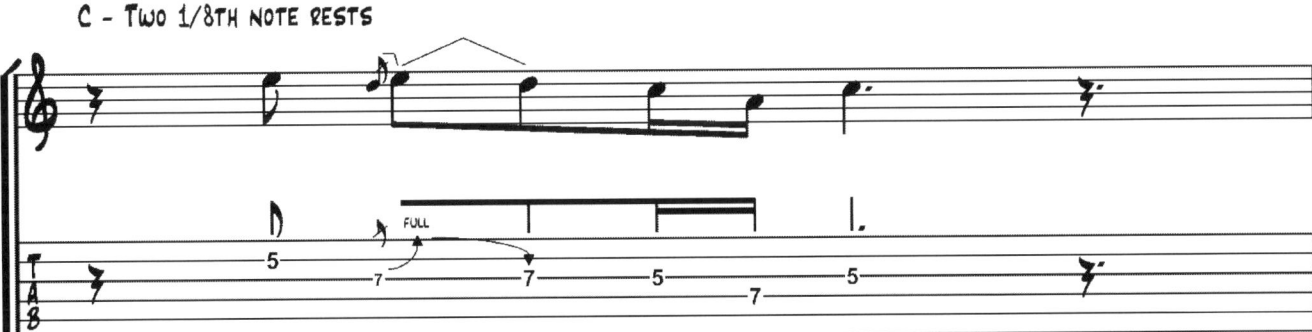

D - One 1/8th note rest and one 1/16th note rest

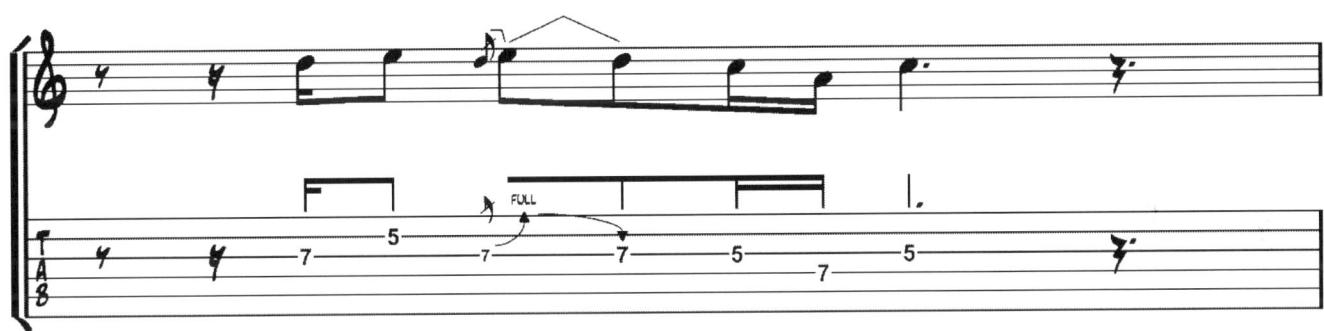

E - One 1/18th Beat Rest

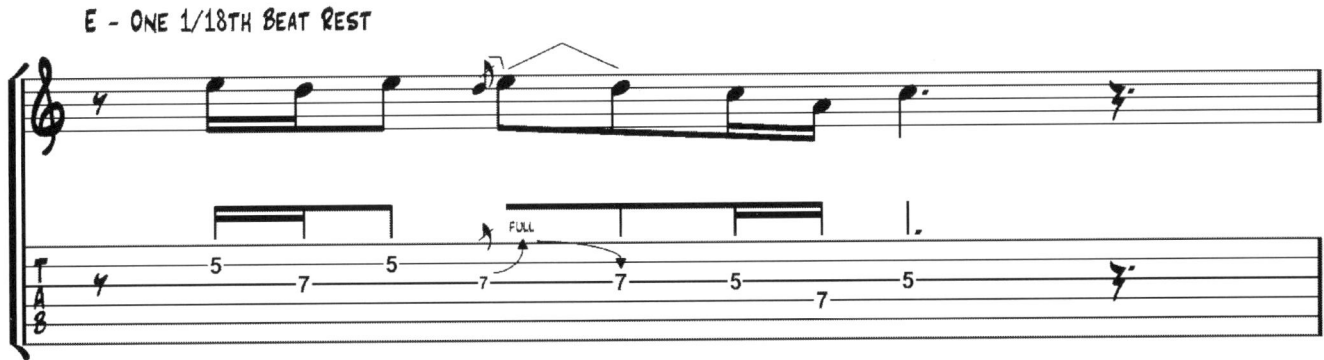

F - ONE 1/16TH NOTE REST

As I'm sure you can hear, using a rest instead of playing a pitch opens up an abundance of melodic options.

In examples 2t (a - f) we simply used varying lengths of rests on beat one of the bar, however we can use rests at *any* point in the bar we choose. We can put a rest on any main beat (Beat 1, 2, 3, or 4) *and/or* on any subdivision of any beat. If I was to go into every possible permutation I would fill many hundreds of pages, so here I will give you some useful ideas to explore in your practice sessions.

Firstly, try using the same approach as on examples 2t (a - f) but apply each differing rest value to the second beat of the bar. You will not be able to use some of the 1/16th note rests because the second beat is comprised mainly of 1/8th notes.

Here are a few ideas to get you started. Don't forget to make them sound vocal by adding in slides and vibrato as soon as you're confident with the rhythms.

Example 2u (a - d):

A — NO REST

B — ONE 1/8TH NOTE REST

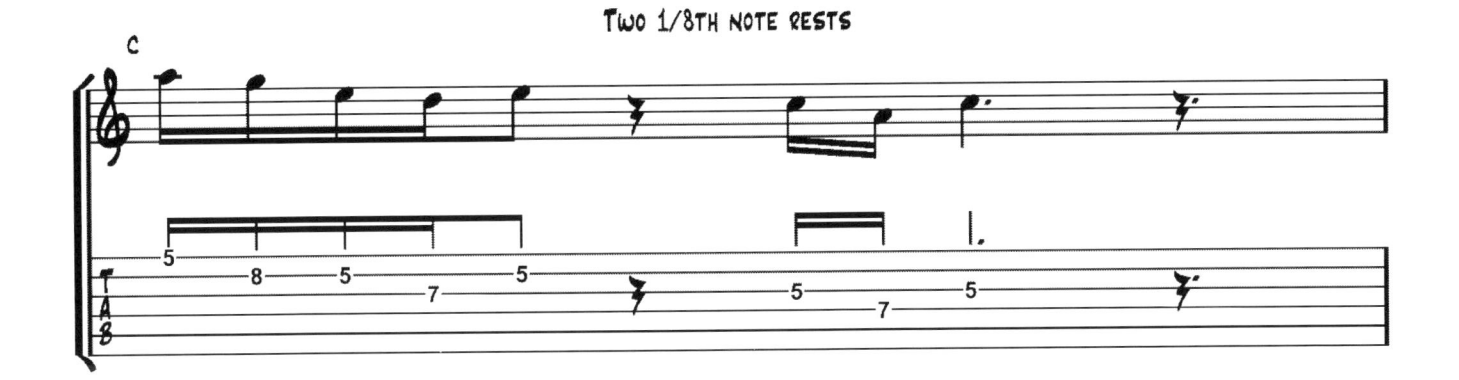

The previous four examples added rests to the start of beat two. We can also add rests to the subdivisions of the beat. Here are some examples that use rests in the *middle* of beat two.

Example 2v (a - c):

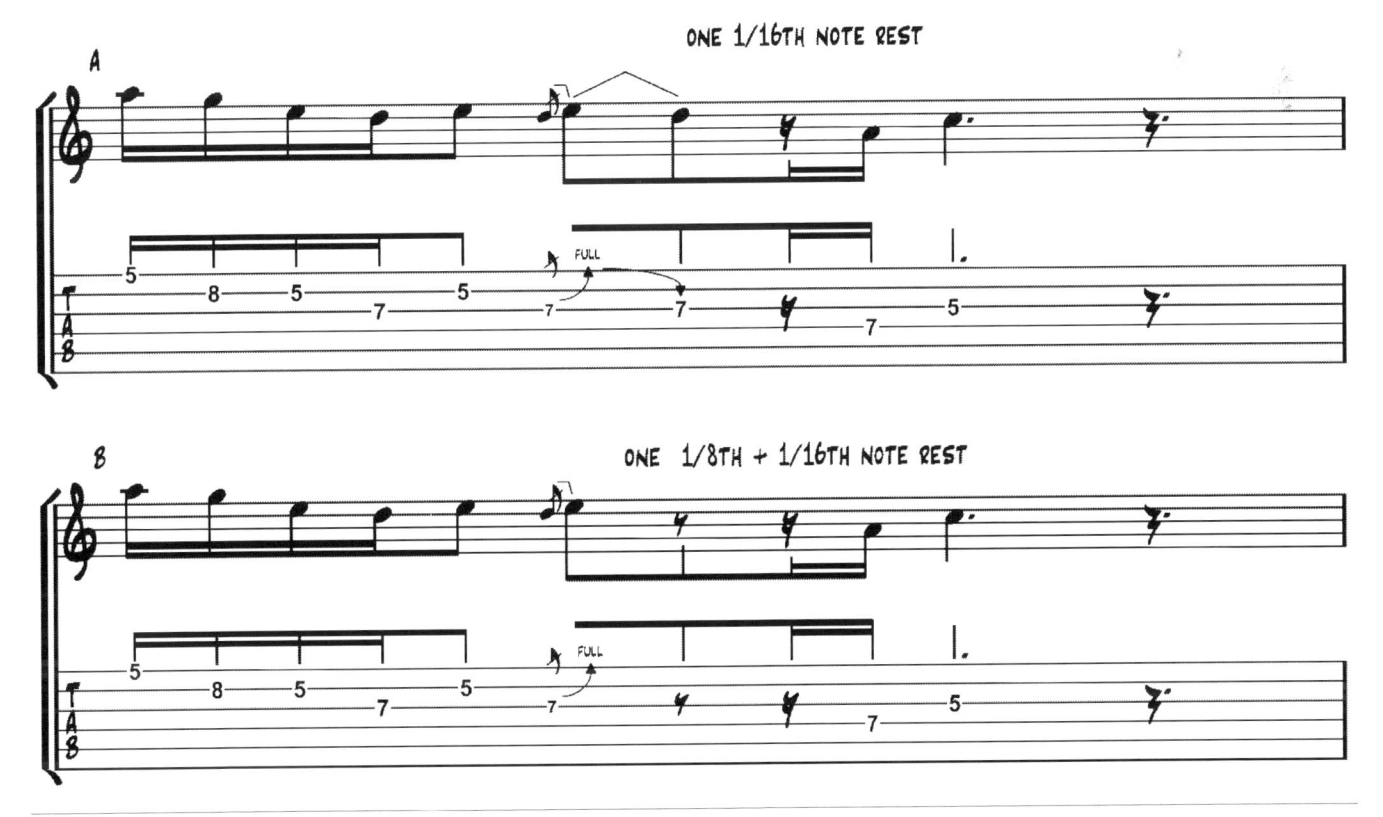

Feel free to let the note preceding a rest ring into the gap if you like the sound of it. Try each example with and without the note ringing, you create very different effects.

We can try adding rests to *both* beat one *and* beat two. This is shown in **Example 2w (a - c):**

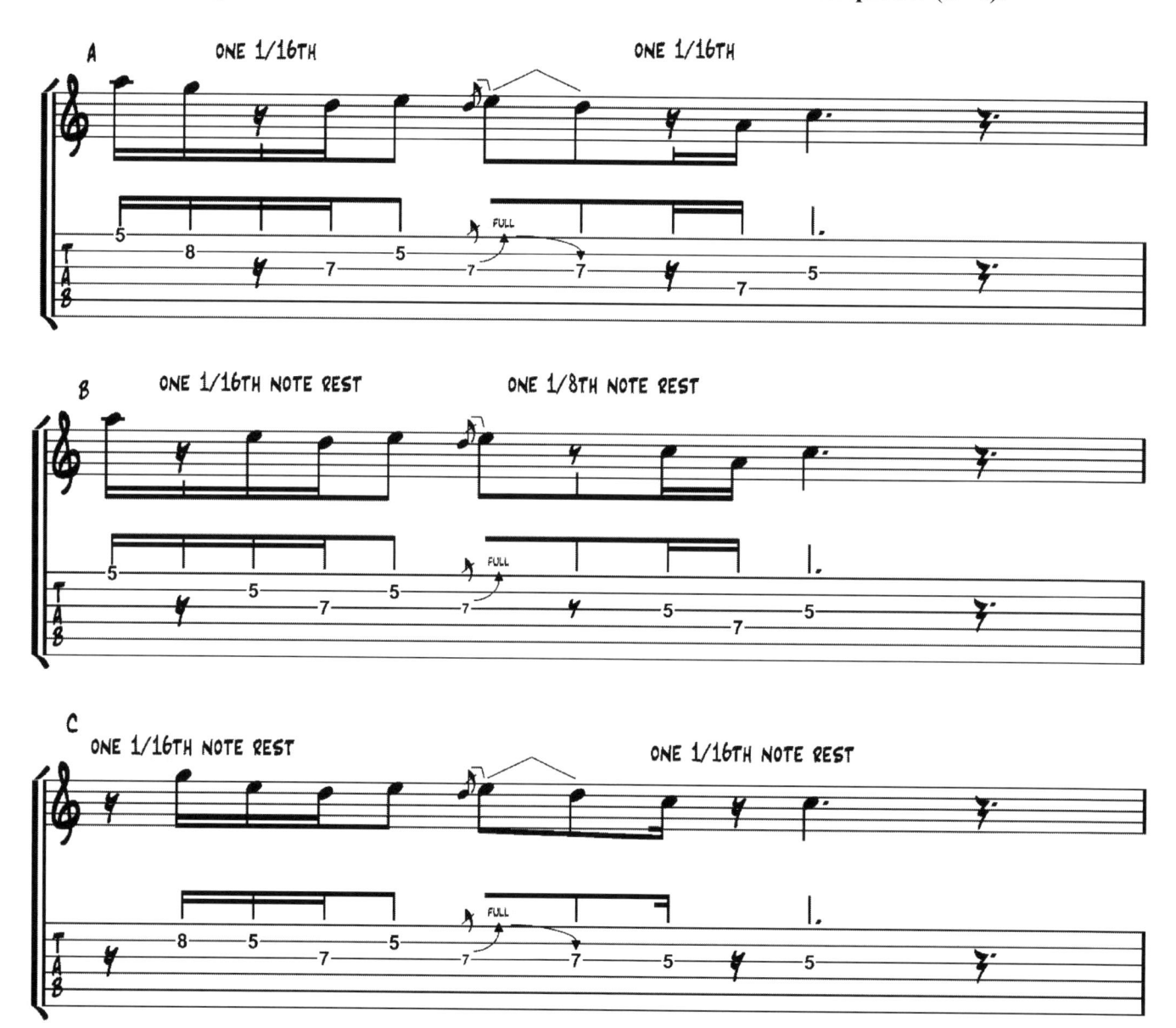

The inclusion of rests or held notes in our playing gives us massive scope to vary our lines and also avoid always beginning each lick on the down-beat.

The final lick above demonstrates this idea by beginning on the second 1/16th note of the bar and creates an interesting *syncopated* effect in the melody line.

I wouldn't go as far as to say "never begin your licks on the beat"; however developing the ability to start from any 1/16th note subdivision of any beat will greatly free up your melodic and expressive technique by helping you control your note placement.

We will study this idea of note placement in great detail in chapter three.

To bring all these ideas into the practice room, begin by taking any two-beat lick from this chapter, for example 2q and arbitrarily add rests to different places in the lick. Begin by adding one rest, then two and maybe even three rests. You can choose the rest values, either one 1/16th, one 1/8th, two 1/8ths or three 1/8ths. Don't forget you can often directly follow a 1/8th rest with a 1/16th rest and vice versa.

Do this with a few of the licks in the book and then try constructing your own from the rhythm chart on page 32.

The point of this exercise is not to see how far you can push the envelope in terms of crazy, disjunct blues phrases (unless those sounds particularly appeal to you). The point is to develop your melodic awareness to encompass rests and breaks in melodic phrases unconsciously. These exercises *are* on the 'academic' side but in order for you to feel the music, the music must first be deconstructed before being built back up in tangible chunks.

So far we have looked at building short lines which last just one or two beats. Try extending these lines to last for three or more beats.

Also: - Listen! Listen to the players that you like. Stevie Ray Vaughan, Jimi Hendrix, Robben Ford, Larry Carlton, Joe Bonamassa, Gary Moore and everyone else play these kinds of rhythms *all the time*. Spend time without your guitar in your hands listening for the spaces in their longer runs.

Soon you will be able to stop constructing lines in this way and just let the music flow but whenever you get stuck in a rut it can be a great idea to simply pick a few rhythms, add the notes and let them feed your melodic creativity.

Duplets (2 against 3 feel)

You may be familiar with the idea of *triplets*. To play a triplet in normal 4/4 time we play three 1/8th notes in the time it normally takes to play two 1/8th notes.

Playing triplet 1/8th notes in 4/4 can (mathematically) give us a similar rhythmic feel to playing 1/8th notes in 12/8.

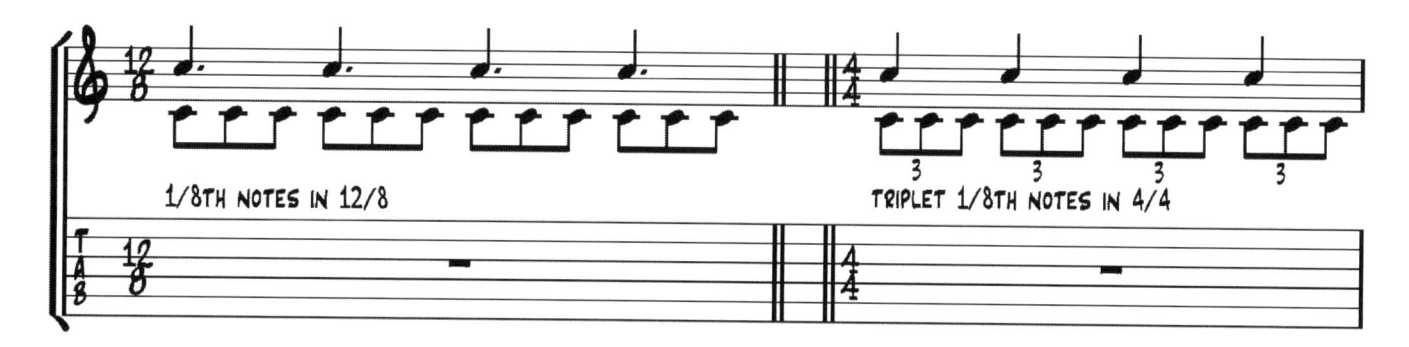

As we are already working in 12/8 and therefore playing in rhythmic groups of three, it is pointless here to study 1/8th note triplets.

It is much more useful to take a look at the 'opposite' of a triplet; a *duplet*. A duplet is simply two 1/8th notes played *evenly* in the time that we would normally play three 1/8th notes:

In this diagram the top line represents the triplet feel of the drums and bass in 12/8 and the bottom line shows how the duplet falls against the triplet.

Example 3a:

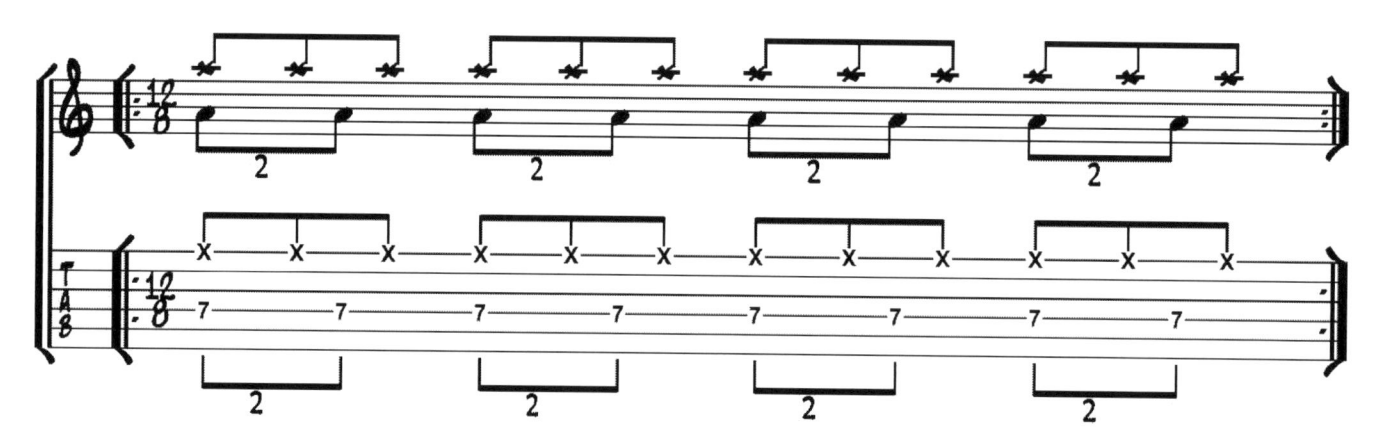

Play through the above example along with the audio example to internalise its rhythm. These kinds of rhythms can be extremely difficult to perform accurately at first, especially at a slow tempo. Try using backing track two or three (medium and fast speeds) when you practice this idea.

The trick I use to stay in time is to 'zone out' of the triplet feel hi-hats in the drum part and focus closely on the bass drum and the snare drum which mark each main pulse in the bar. I *always* tap my foot with these drums and then count out loud "one and two and three and four and…" This makes it a lot easier to divide the beat in two by helping to remove the distraction of the hi-hats.

Once you have this feel clear in your mind, try playing an ascending A minor pentatonic scale using duplets against backing track one:

Example 3b:

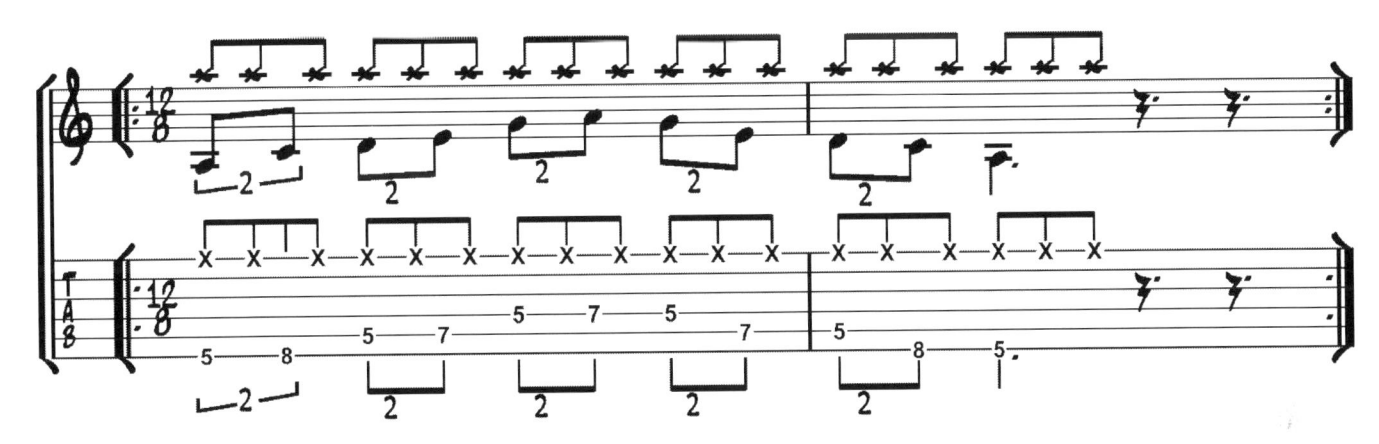

While these duplets are useful, I have always found it much more efficient to practice 'doubling up' the 1/8th note duplets into 1/16th notes. These are a much more common rhythmic division in a 12/8 blues.

4 against 3 1/16th notes look like this on paper:

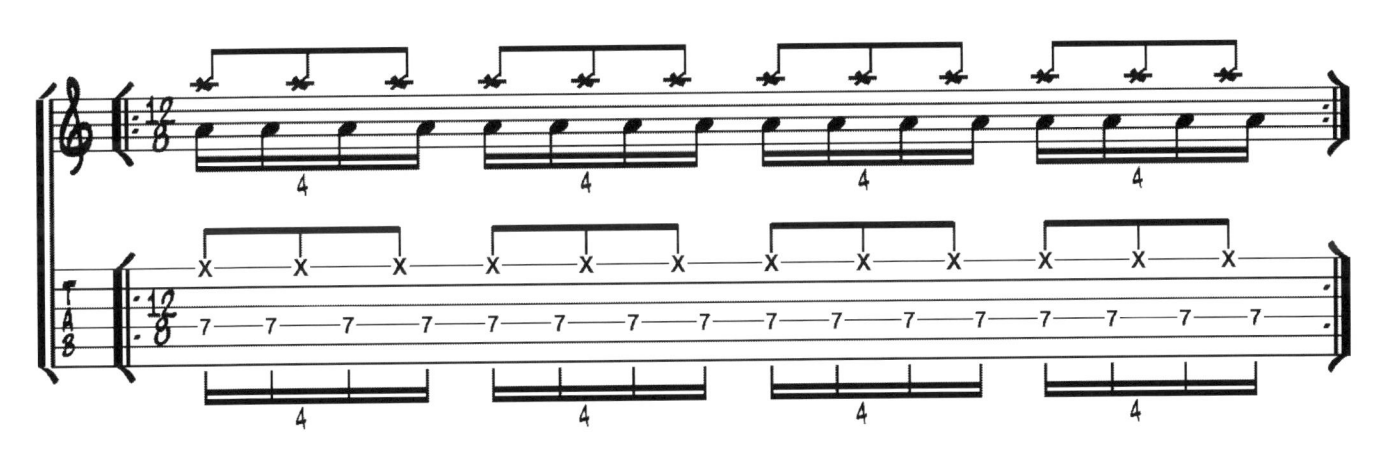

Practice this idea in the same way as described for the duplets. Focus on the kick and snare drum and try to ignore the hi-hats. Duplet 1/16th notes are a lot easier to hear and play than the duplet 1/8ths.

Again try playing the pentatonic scale ascending and descending in this rhythm against the triplet backing track.

Example 3c:

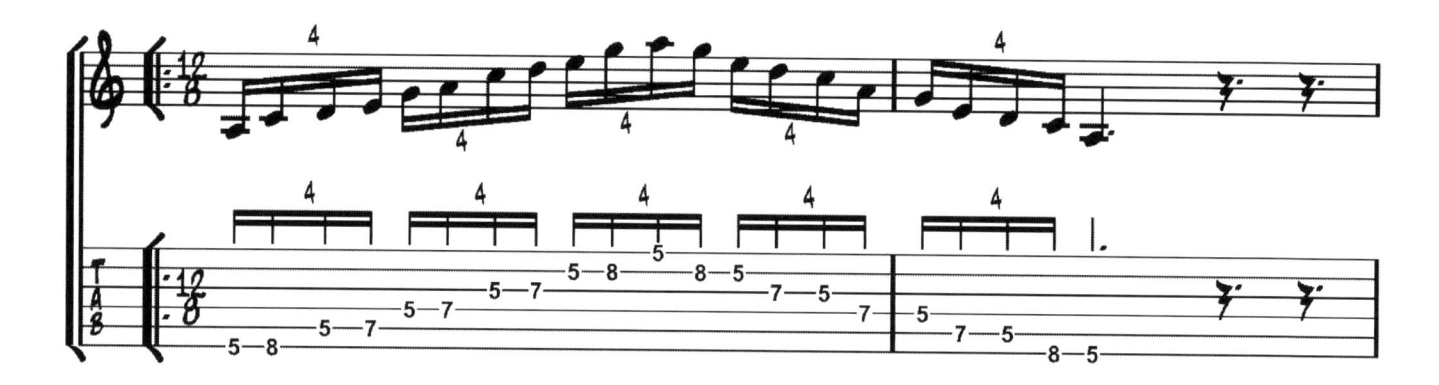

Now practice moving between a normal triplet feel and the 1/16th note duplets:

Example 3d:

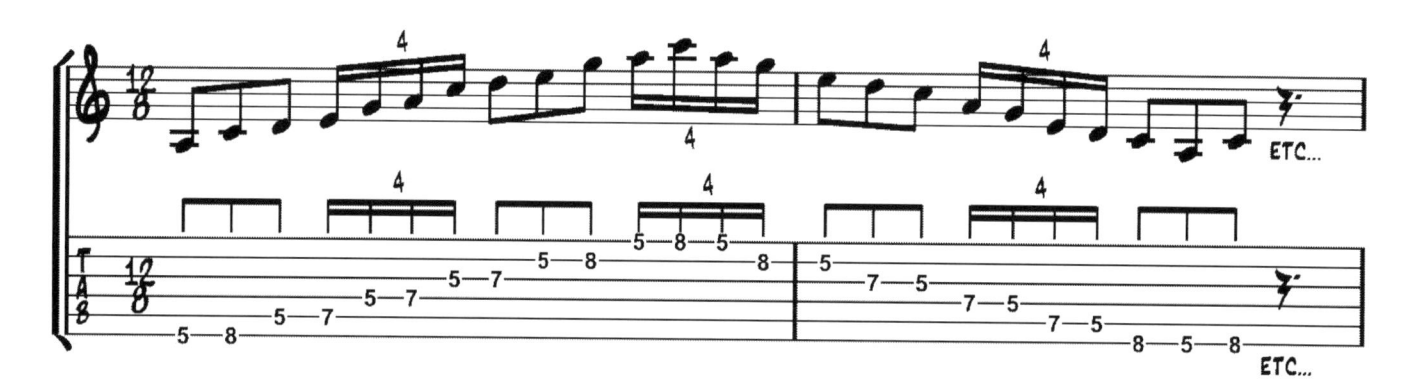

Finally, learn these lines which combine both normal and duplet notes. Play along with the audio examples and be careful to match the phrasing exactly.

Example 3e:

Example 3f:

Example 3g:

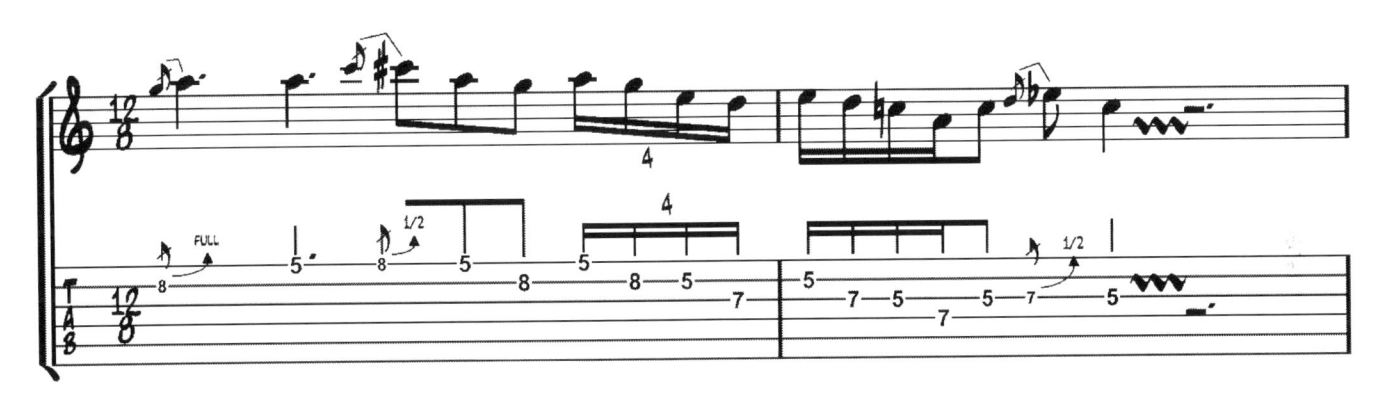

In example 3g, notice how I use notes of decreasing value to give the effect of speeding up throughout the lick. The rhythmic tension of the duplet 1/16th notes is resolved by the normal 1/16ths in bar two.

These examples are just the tip of the iceberg, but if you've ever wondered how your favourite players get that 'straining against the beat' feel, this is one of the main ways of creating rhythmic, as opposed to melodic tension.

Another reminder! - These licks are simply written as 'dots on paper'. If I was to include every little slide, curl, vibrato and other nuance in my playing it would be very difficult to read. A large part of your practice should be to work on making these lines come alive with these kinds of expressive techniques.

Chapter 3: Rhythmic Displacement

In chapter two we examined how we could insert silence into a blues lick by using a rest. This rest could either have the function of creating a rhythmic 'hole' in the lick, or it could remove the first couple of notes from the line and make it seem like it was starting later.

In this chapter we will be looking at how we can move a *whole* phrase across different beats of the bar and we will discover the interesting and useful musical effects of doing so.

Displacement on the Beat

We will begin as always with a very simple example. Here is a six note phrase that begins on beat one of the bar.

Example 3h:

Play this line over backing track one and be sure to begin it each time on beat one.

Now let's move this line to the right by one beat and start it on beat two.

Example 3i:

Be very careful to ensure you are actually playing example 3i on beat *two* of the bar. When I teach this concept to private students I have them count out loud "One, Two, Three, Four, One" before beginning on beat two to help them develop awareness of the point in the bar at which they're 'placing' the lick. Listen carefully to the audio example as this is a crucial concept to grasp.

In example 3i we used an idea called *rhythmic displacement*. In other words, we took a single phrase and *displaced* it so it began later in the bar. In this example, by beginning the lick one beat later we leave a rhythmic 'breath' at the start of the bar and switch up our playing by making our phrasing less predictable.

You may not notice at first but you are actually subtly altering the musical *effect* this simple lick has on your listener. Different notes/intervals fall at different points in the bar giving a subtly altered flavour to the line. This is a fairly easy way to reuse material without it being completely obvious. Moreover, learning to play from any point in the bar is obviously an essential step towards mastering your timing, rhythm and phrasing.

Next, let's see what happens if we move this phrase another beat to the right and begin playing on beat *three*.

Example 3j:

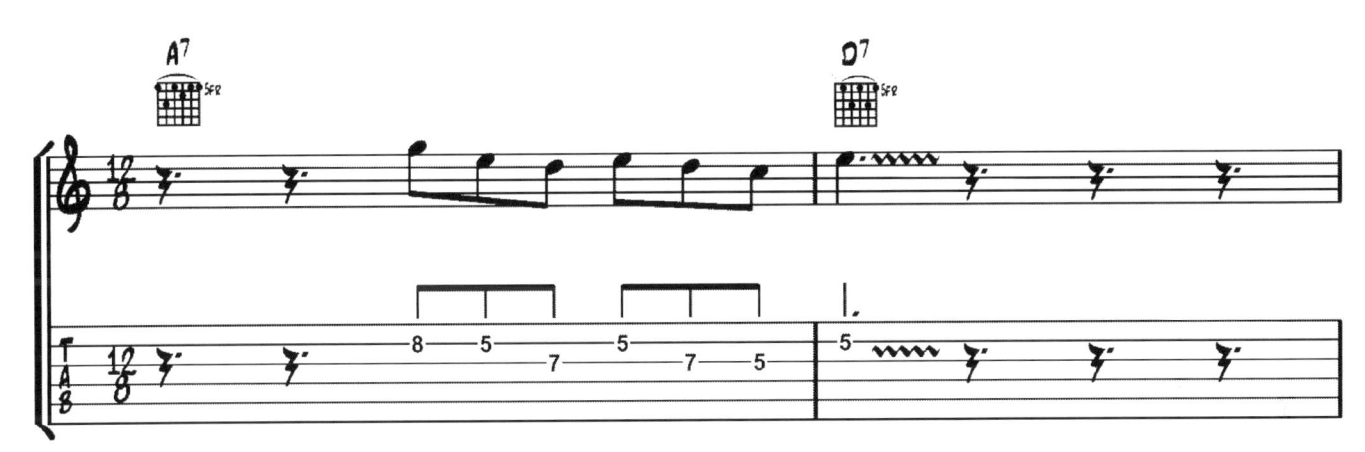

Again, practice counting in before playing your line. You might wish to start counting in the preceding bar and say out loud "One, Two, Three, Four, One, Two" and then start the lick on beat three.

On one level, this is great practice for controlling your phrasing. How often until this point have you actually been *aware* of when/where in the bar you are starting your line? This kind of heightened consciousness can quickly be revolutionary in many students' playing.

On another, more profound level, something very interesting has happened to the way this phrase *feels* musically. By starting on beat three in this way the final note, (E) no longer falls on the A7 chord in bar one: It falls on the D7 chord in bar two. The note (E) is now heard in a different *context* from before because the harmony has changed beneath it.

If you're up on your music theory, you may understand when the note E falls on the A7 it functions as the 'stable' 5th of the chord, however when the E falls with a D7 chord playing underneath it as above then the E note forms the slightly 'tense' 9th in the scale. The best way to hear and understand this effect is simply to listen carefully to the lick in context.

Listen again to example 3i and then immediately listen to example 3j. Can you hear the subtle difference in the 'meaning' of the phrase?

As I mentioned before this is a great and common way to 'recycle' your melodic material (licks). The line in 3i sounds completely different than the line in 3j and it is very hard for the listener to consciously distinguish their similarities, even when they're played right next to each other! In fact what happens is that the listener subconsciously hears that these phrases are linked in some way and gets the feeling that the music is well constructed.

Let's try this lick beginning from beat four. Remember to count out loud to help ensure your accuracy.

Example 3k:

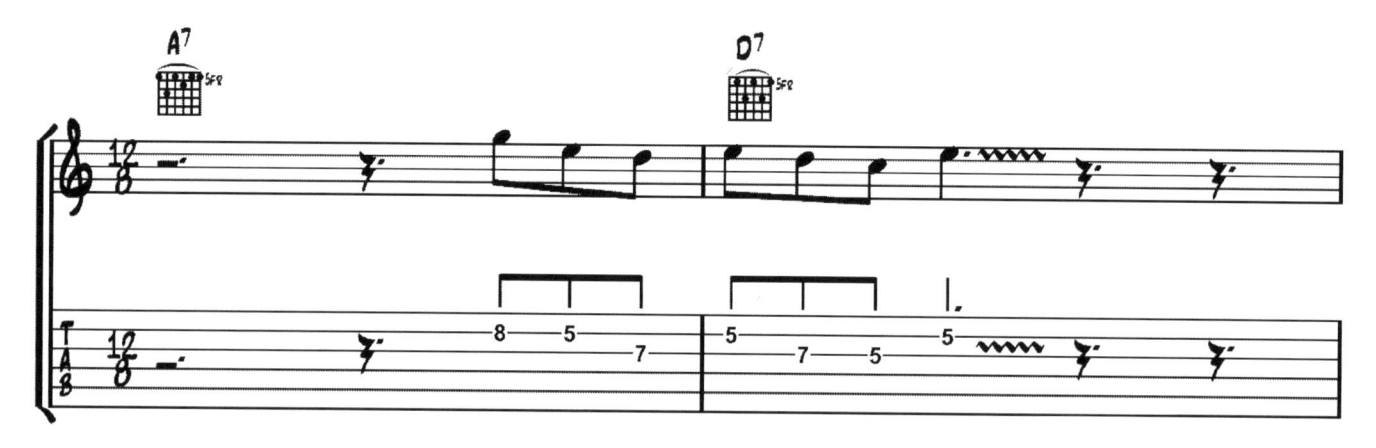

This time the line sounds very different as more than half of the notes fall on the D7 chord as opposed to the A7 chord.

Of course, the harmony/chords in a blues tune does not change *every* bar however, if you can learn to time your licks to overlap a bar line when the chord *does* change then you will develop some very interesting results.

To refresh your memory, here is a full (simple) 12 bar blues progression chord chart. Use it to locate areas where you can play this six note lick in the second half of the bar to cross the bar line and 'hit' a chord change. Listen carefully to the effect this creates.

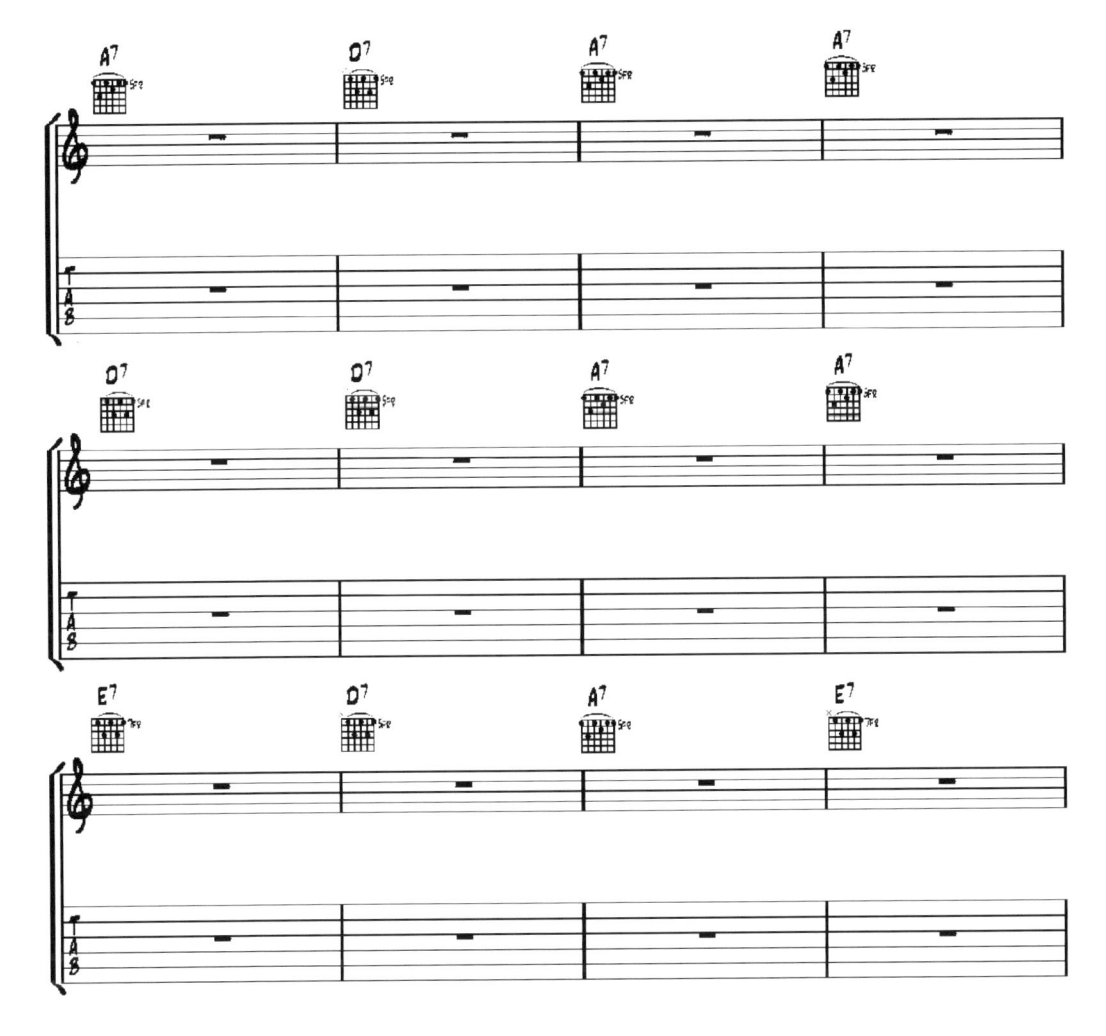

Play the following exercises to develop your control of rhythmic development along with backing track one.

Take one short blues lick that is 4 or 5 notes long; maybe something like *example 2i (b)* on page 26.

1) Play the lick (and *only* the lick!) beginning on beat one of each bar for a **full 12 bar chorus**.
2) Next use the same lick but beginning each time on beat *two* of each bar.
3) Now begin the same line on beat three of each bar. A line longer than two beats will start to cross the bar line at this point.
4) Begin on beat four of the bar. Remember to repeat each exercise for a *whole chorus* of blues backing.
5) Now try playing through a complete chorus but begin the line on beat one in the first bar, beat two in the second, three in the third and four in the fourth. Don't play in the fifth bar because the line in bar four will have carried over the bar line, but begin again by playing the lick on beat one in the sixth bar. Keep this process going for as long as you can.
6) Try reversing the pattern by starting on beat four in bar one, and then beat three in bar two etc.

These exercises will help you develop controlled placement of all of your musical vocabulary.

Displacement by 1/8th Note Divisions of the Beat

The following section is one of my favourite lessons to teach. This lesson is often where the student 'gets' the whole concept of musical placement and suddenly understands why we *don't* need ten thousand blues licks to play creatively, emotively and effectively. I've seen these ideas completely transform many students' playing in minutes, often with astonishing results.

In the previous section we looked at how we could take a musical phrase and displace it to begin later in the bar by moving it *one beat* at a time. Now we will study how to take a phrase and rhythmically displace it by *one 1/8th note* each time.

By displacing a lick by 1/8th notes we can *completely* change the musical effect of a lick so we can easily manipulate identical licks to make them sound and feel very different.

We will begin with a short, 1/8th note phrase like this.

Example 3l:

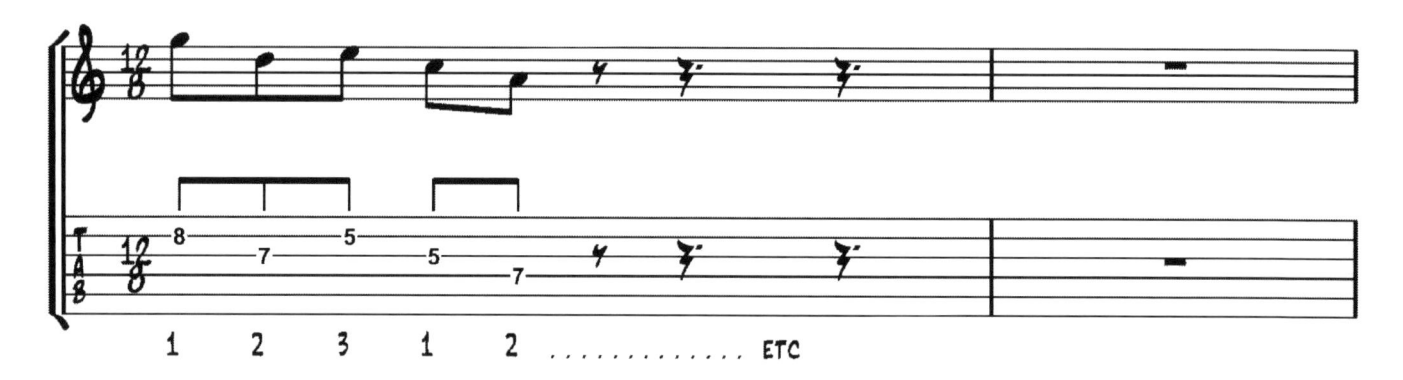

Play this along with backing track one and *count out loud* each 1/8th note division. As you play say

"One two three one two three one two three one two three" as shown below example 3l.

We will now rhythmically displace this phrase one 1/8th note to the right. Listen to the profound effect this displacement has on the melody.

Example 3m:

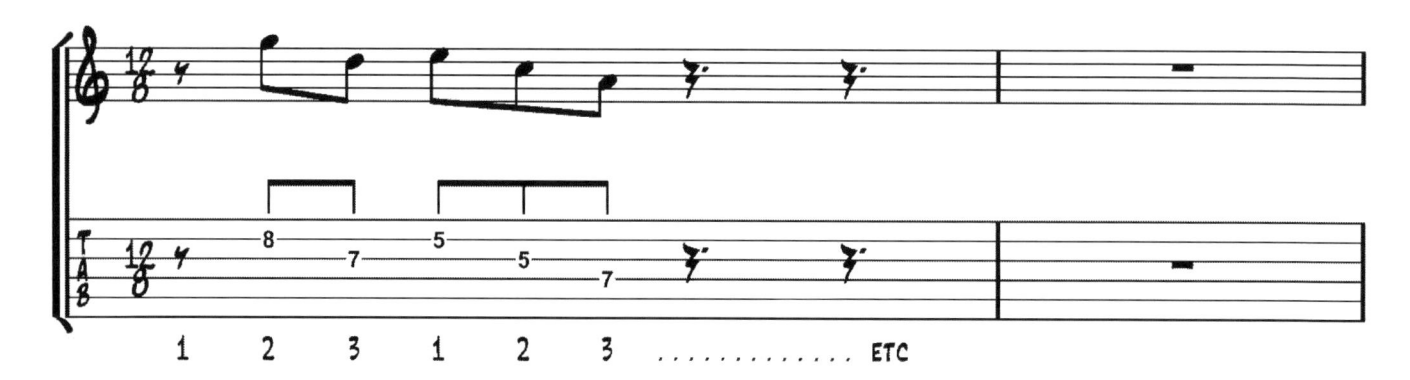

It helps a great deal at first to be counting out loud as you play these examples. As you play through more examples they will become second nature and you will not have to count any more.

There are two reasons that example 3m sounds quite so different from example 3l. Firstly as we discussed previously, the individual pitches fall at slightly different times in the bar which will subtly alter their 'flavour', but there is another much more intrinsic reason for their difference.

Certain rhythmic points in *any* bar of music are subtly accented to create musical *feel* and momentum. The specific parts of the bar that are accented vary from style to style and from time signature to time signature. The precise accents are hard to pin down, but as a *very* general rule, the down beats in modern music are *strong* (beats one, two three and four) with beats two and four being more accented than beats one and three.

In addition, the first and third 1/8th notes in each bar are often given a slight natural accent.

All these factors combine so that by simply displacing the lick by one 1/8th note, different parts of the phrase fall on different strong or accented parts of the bar.

Using rhythmic displacement in this way can completely disguise a line from your audience because they will hear different notes (scale intervals) falling on different parts (rhythmic accents) of the bar. They may consciously or unconsciously hear the same melodic *shape*, but unless they are quite well musically trained they will not spot a rhythmic displacement unless you make it extremely obvious.

Assuming that your audience know what a rhythmic displacement is, are listening for it, or even care, if they recognise that you used the same line twice albeit slightly differently, the most common reaction you will get is 'cool!'

Now let's try moving this phrase onto the third 1/8th note of beat one.

Example 3n:

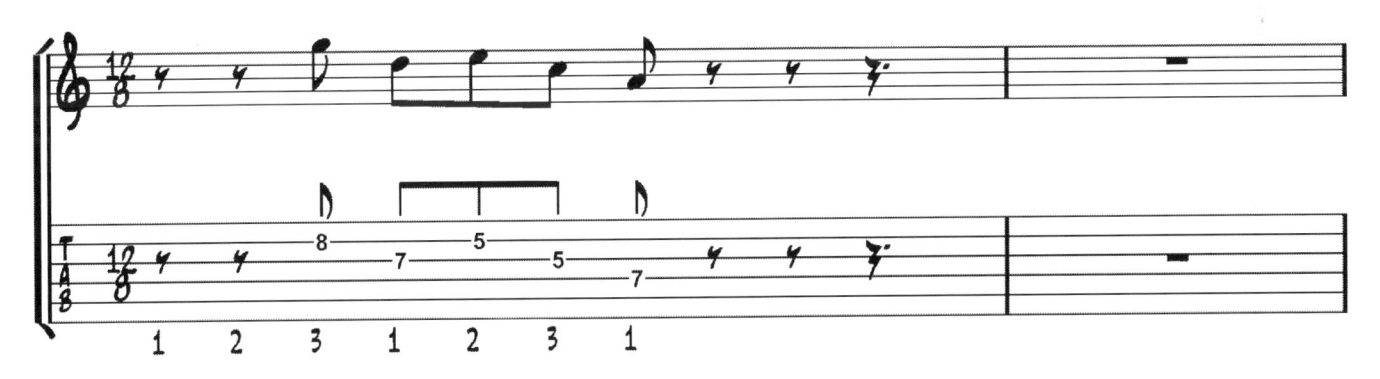

Make sure you're counting the 1/8th notes to ensure you start the lick at the correct point.

Once again, the phrase *feels* completely different. Instead of being a line that is based around the first beat of the bar, it has suddenly become focused on the second and third beats. In this version the accents fall on the second and final notes of the lick changing it to become almost unrecognisable.

Of course, we can continue to move this line one 1/8th note to the right each time and create an altered phrase each time. Things really start to become interesting when this kind of displacement starts to cross the bar line. We can achieve this by beginning the lick on the second 1/8th note of beat three.

Example 3o:

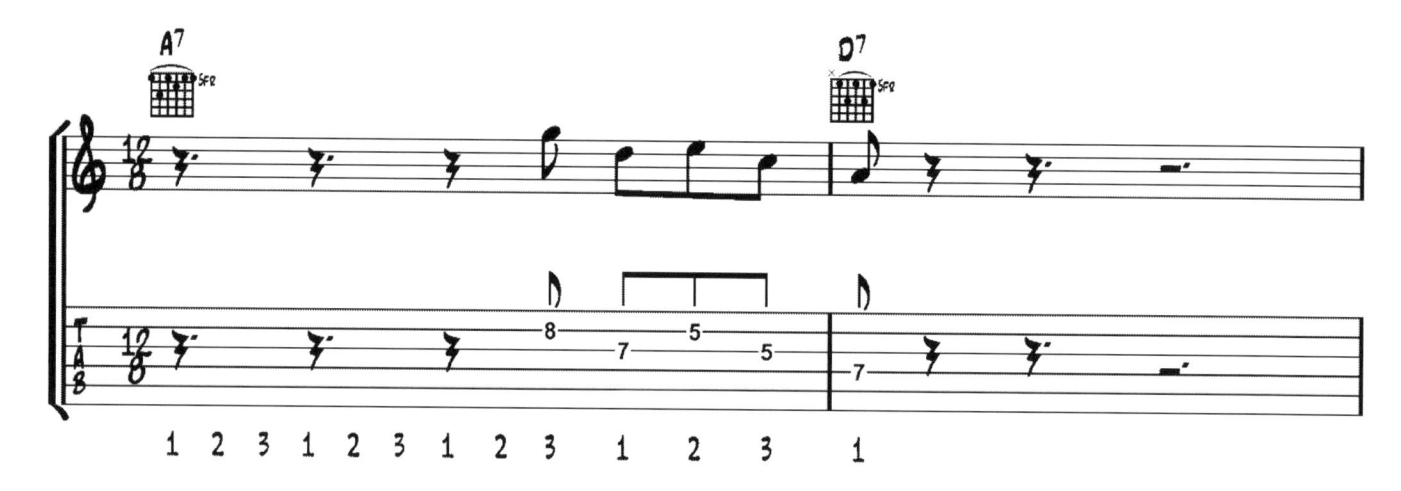

As with example 3j earlier, you can hear that the final note of example 3o now 'functions' differently from example 3n. The final note now falls on the D7 chord creating a huge difference in the melodic effect of the lick.

We can start this line at any point from beat four and cross the bar line by a few notes. Listen to, and play the following examples to get a feel for moving these displaced licks further across the bar line.

Example 3p (a):

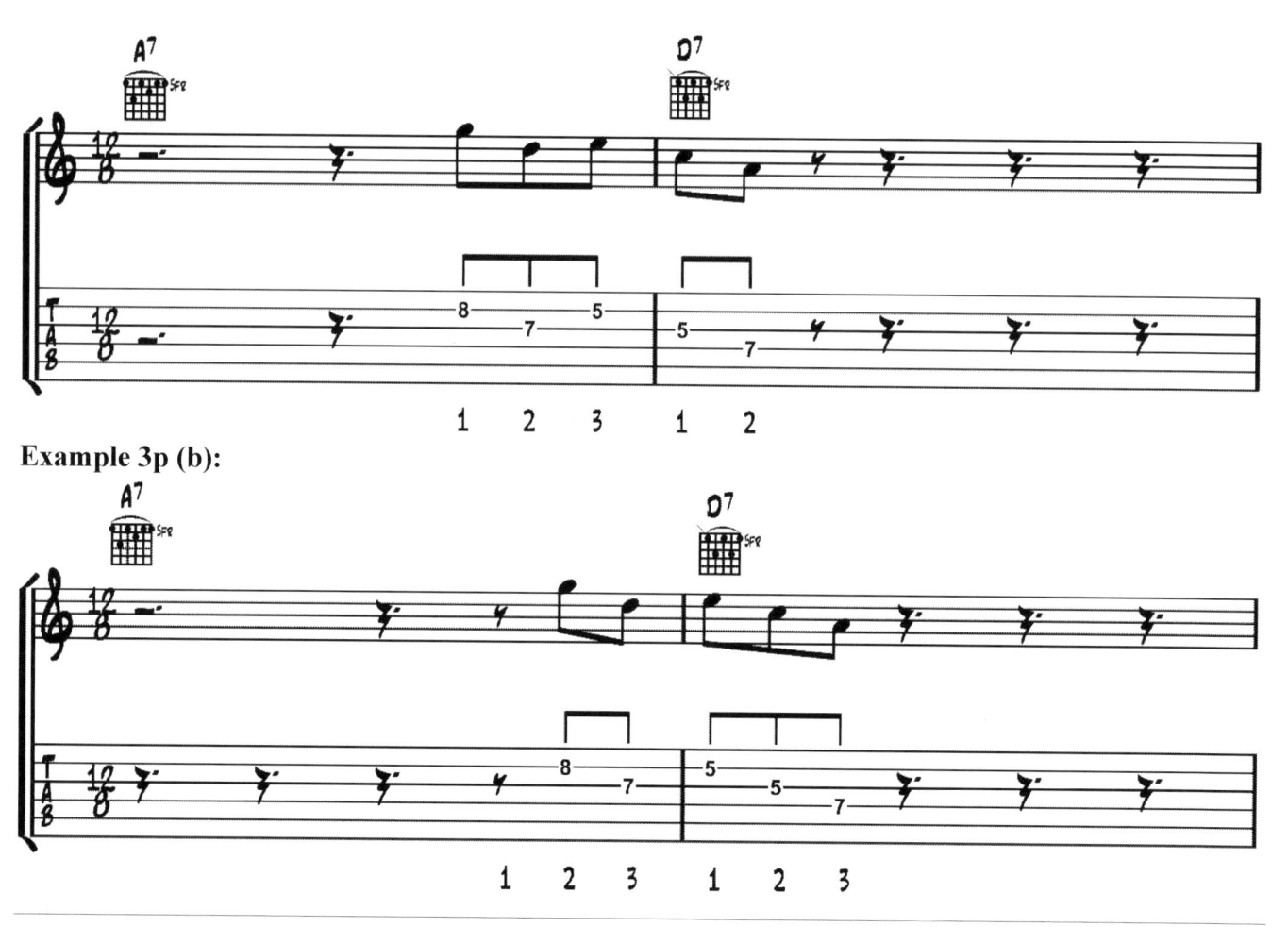

Example 3p (b):

50

Example 3p (c):

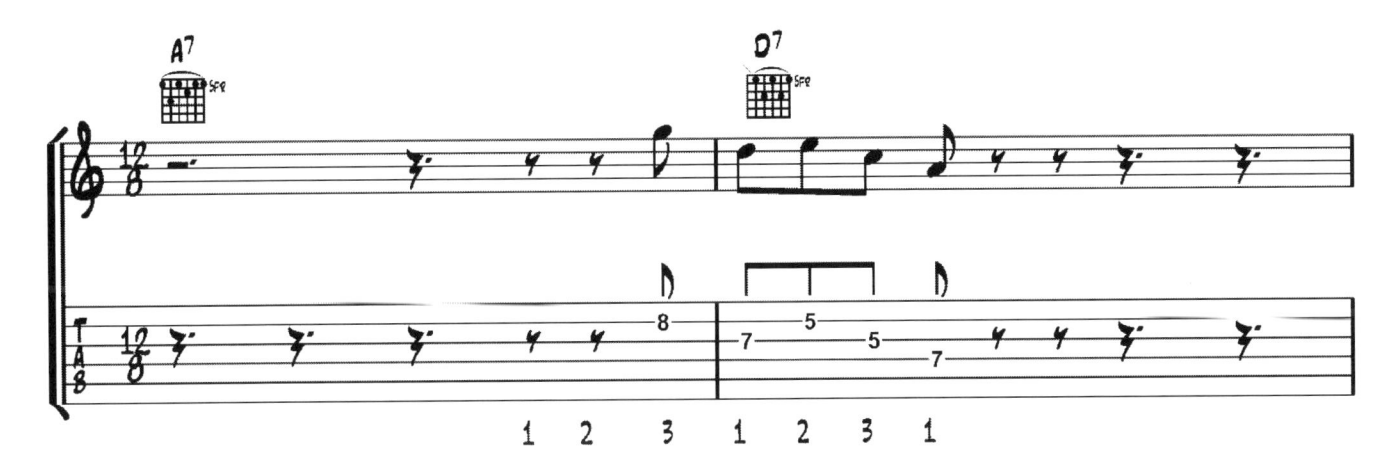

As I'm sure you can hear, these three lines all feel unique even though we are actually playing the same sequence of notes. The key to unlocking this powerful technique is to learn to be in control of exactly where you begin your line.

To develop your rhythmic placement repeat the exercise on page 47, however instead of shifting your line by a whole beat each time, just shift it by one 1/8th note.

1) Choose a short line based around 1/8th notes, maybe something like example 2k b, c or d.
2) Play through one chorus beginning this line on the first 1/8th note of bar one.
3) Repeat this lick on the second chorus but begin on the *second* 1/8th note of beat one.
4) Now begin the line on the *third* 1/8th note of beat one.
5) Keep moving the line one 1/8th note to the right until you reach the third 1/8th note of beat four.
6) Try playing a few choruses and shift the line one 1/8th note to the right *each bar*.

If you struggle playing a whole phrase at first, begin by simply trying to place a single note or muted strum at the designated place in the bar. This will quickly develop your rhythmic awareness.

Important 'big picture' point!

The rhythmic techniques above are not only essential in opening up the bar for you; there is a *major* benefit to practicing in this way.

One of the best models for creating memorable and melodic blues solos is the 'call and response' or 'question and answer' approach to phrasing which goes right back to the 'field hollers' and spirituals that I mentioned in chapter one of this book, and wrote about extensively in the introduction to book one of this series.

Imagine for a minute that the phrases you have been working on are the *questions* in that model. If we can create 12 subtly different questions from just one phrase you are giving yourself the opportunity to let your creativity flow and answer these questions in many possible ways.

Picking a number out of thin air, let's say that off the top of your head you can improvise eight answers to any melodic question. Well now you have twelve different sounding questions from just one phrase and ninety-six possible answers!

Obviously musical creativity doesn't work in such a literal sense, but what I'm trying to demonstrate is that by playing a 'set up' lick in many different ways you will spontaneously generate hundreds of possible, individual and unique answers.

We will be studying the question and answer concept much more deeply in chapter four.

Displacement by 1/16th Note Divisions of the Beat

Displacing a phrase by a 1/16th note is quite a lot harder than displacing a phrase by a 1/8th or whole beat, however when we have mastered this kind of precise placement, our rhythmic perception rockets into uncharted territory. We are essentially giving ourselves the opportunity to begin the same lick at up to twenty-four different places in the bar. Don't panic though; we have already covered twelve of them in the previous two sections!

One of the trickiest challenges when displacing by 1/16th notes is that any line that begins with an 1/8th note will generally be fairly tricky to play at first. It's definitely worth working on though and we will discuss that later. For now, let's begin with a line that begins with some 1/16th notes.

Example 3q:

By now you know the process so let's displace this line one 1/16th note to the right:

Example 3r:

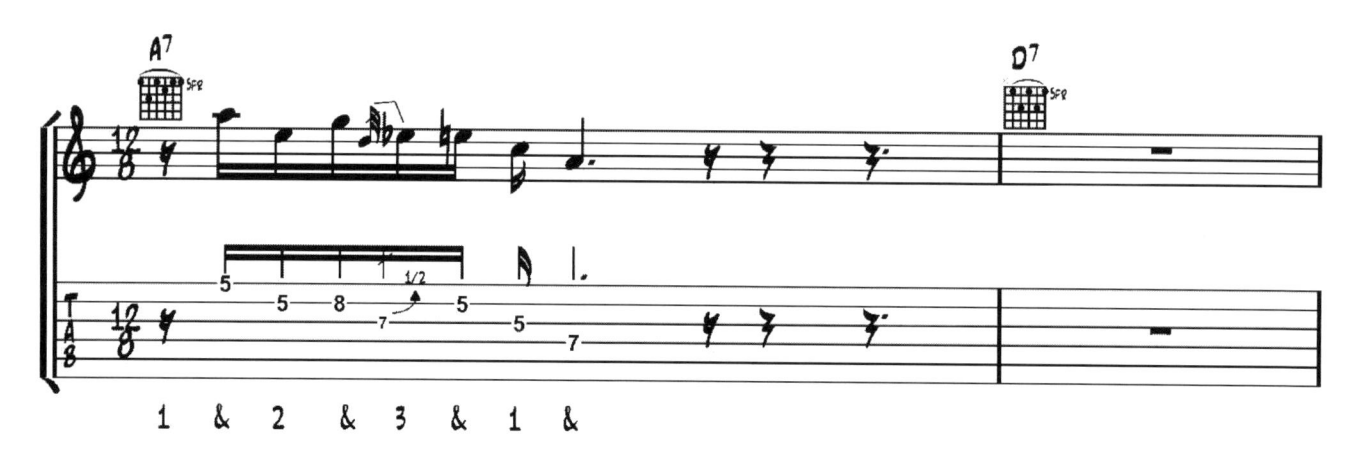

Play this first displacement throughout a whole chorus of 12 bar blues.

Now practice displacing this lick one 1/16th note later (to the right) and playing each displacement for a full chorus before moving on to the next.

When you move the previous example to begin one 1/16th note later you will be starting the line on the *second* 1/8th note of beat one which was covered in example 3m. You should however still practice this line beginning from the second 1/8th note of beat one because this line uses 1/16th notes and will feel different to play.

The displacements for the remaining permutations on beat one are as follows:

Example 3s (a):

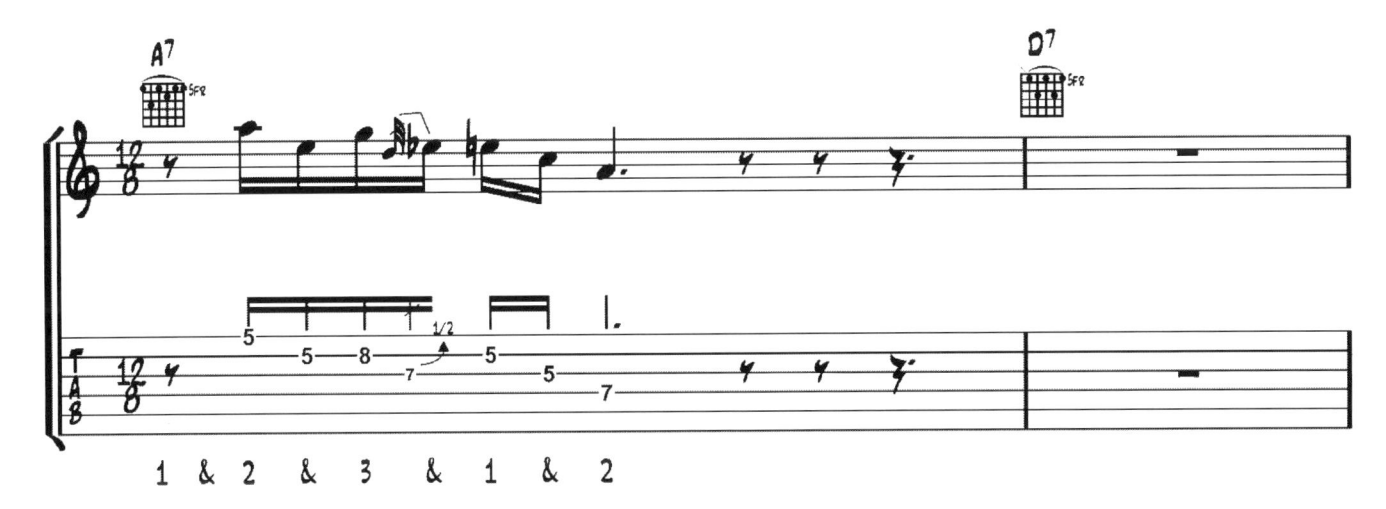

Example 3s (b):

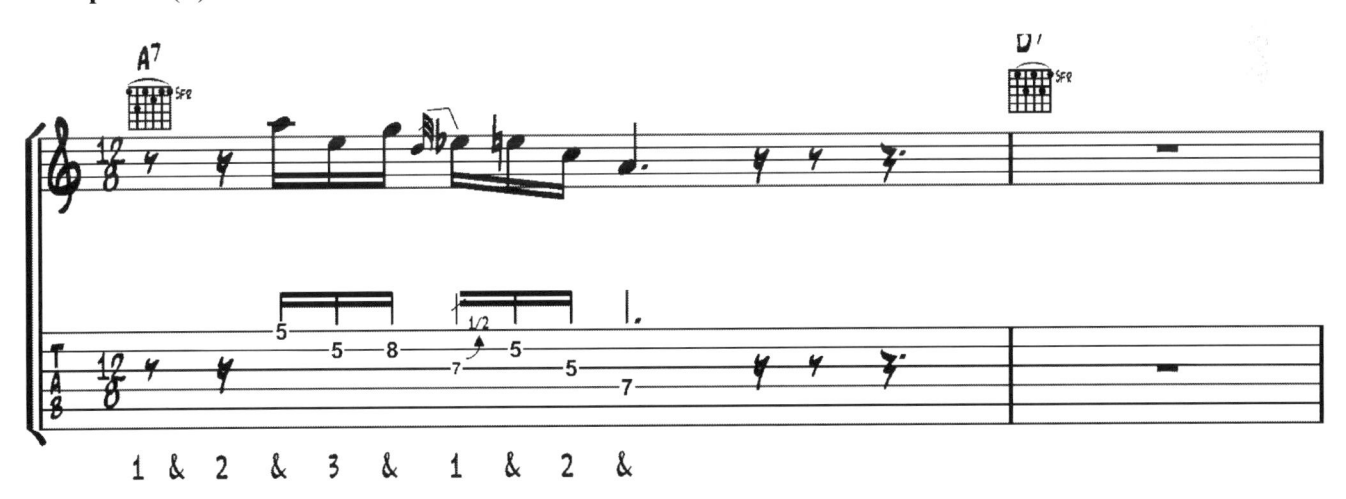

53

Example 3s (c):

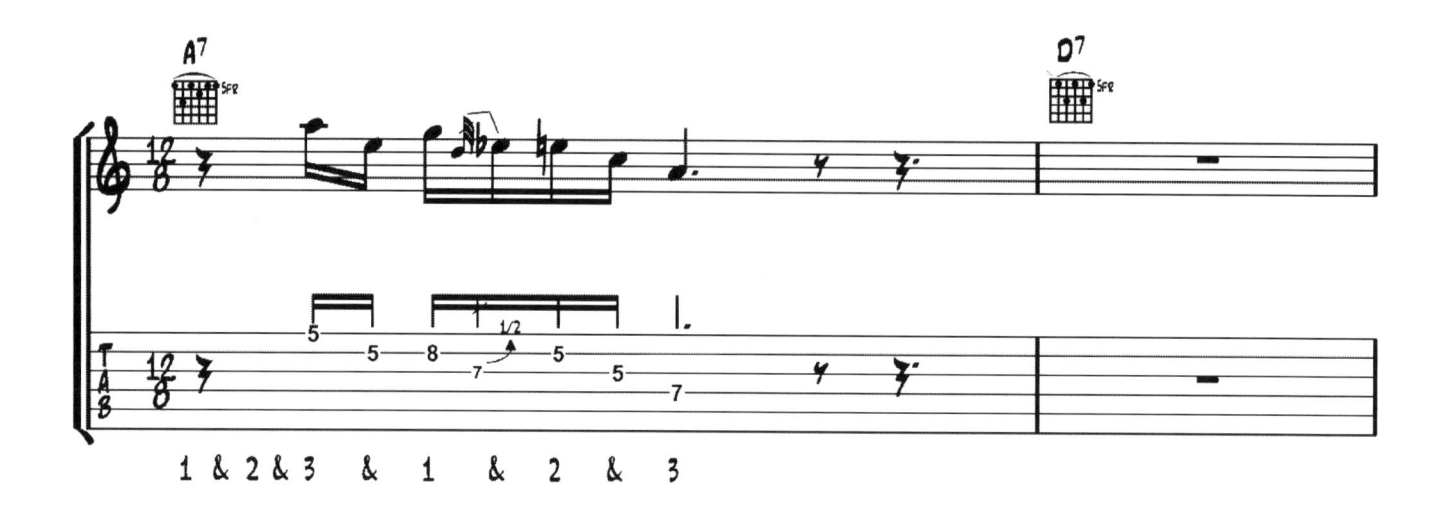

Example 3s (d):

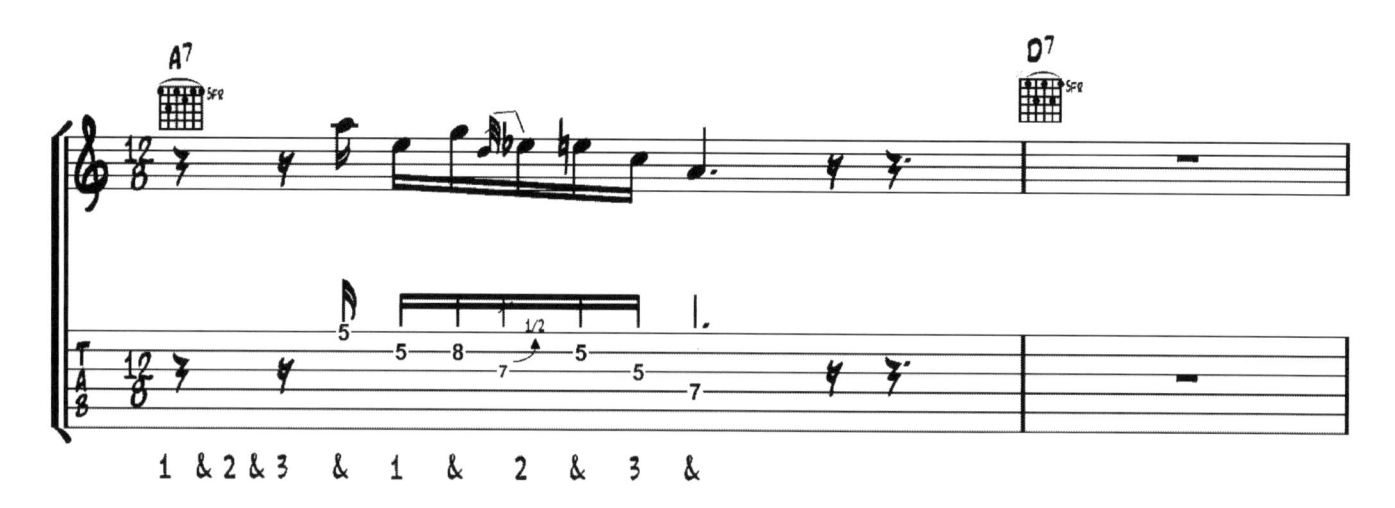

Keep moving the lick back by one 1/16th note in each successive chorus. Listen to how playing the lick over the chord change completely alters the sound of this line when you start placing the line on beat four.

Displacements with 1/16ths are harder than displacements with 1/8ths so take your time and pay careful attention to the audio examples to make sure you are getting it right.

Try coming up with a few other 1/16th note licks and then displace them by the same process.

The complication comes when we displace a lick which contains 1/8th notes by one 1/16th note because it will often cause the 1/8th note to 'cross' a beat. These examples can look a little complex on paper when we displace them but each note in the phrase always lasts the same amount of time.

Learn the following simple 1/8th note line.

Example 3t:

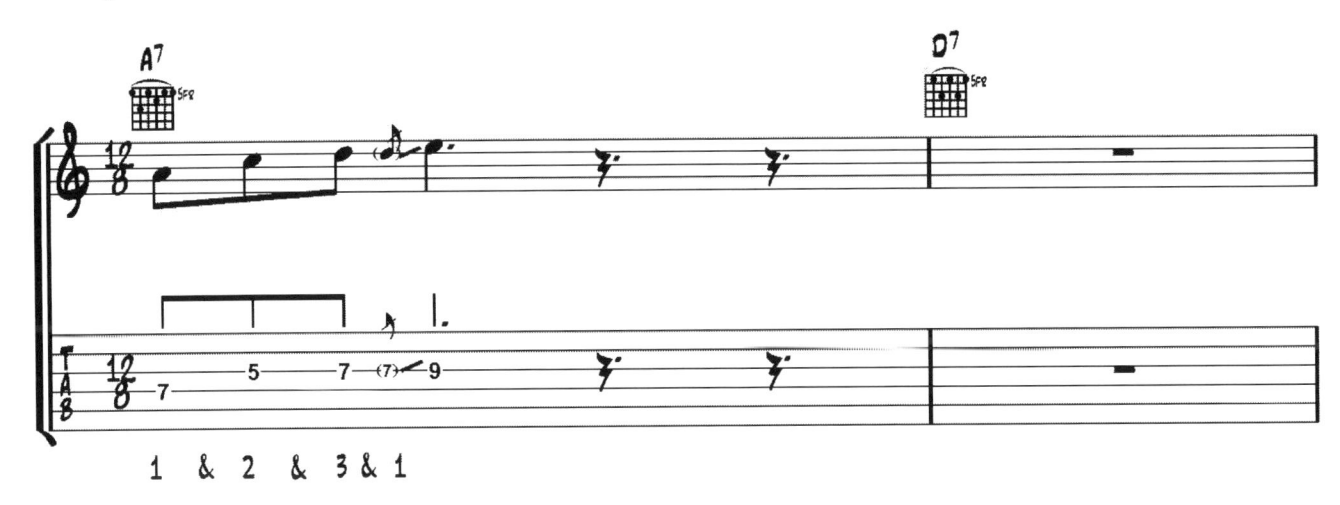

When we displace this lick by 1/16th note to the right it can be very difficult to feel how long each 1/8th note should actually last for. This is the 'correct' notation for the 1/16th note displacement:

Example 3u:

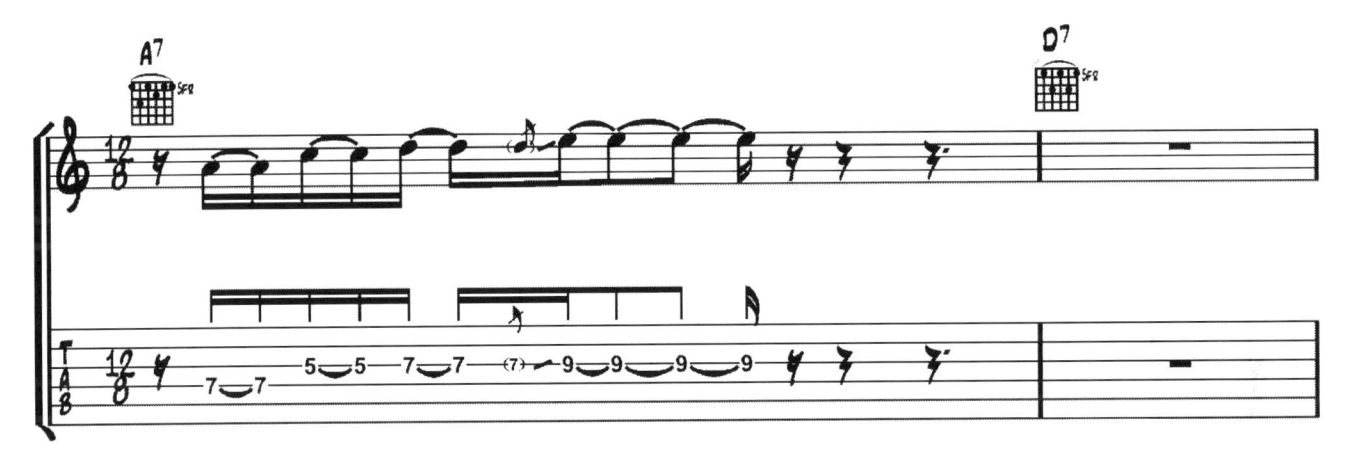

If this looks a little daunting just remember that two 1/16th notes tied together last the same amount of time as one 1/8th note.

You may wish to see the lick like this:

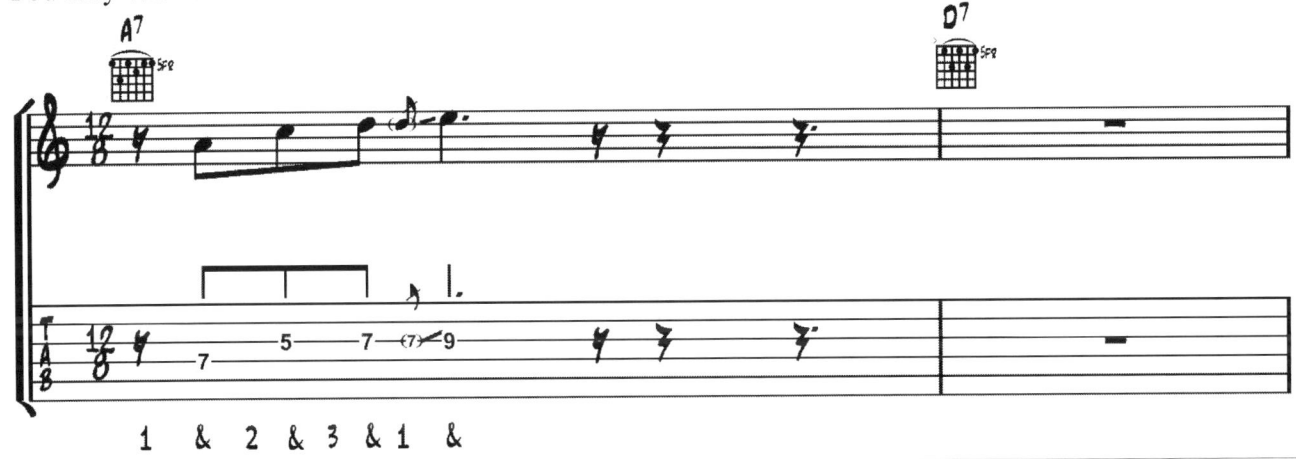

55

Although according to standard musical convention this notation is incorrect, it does make it easier to read the line. The previous two examples are identical.

To internalise the rhythmic feel of a line like this, I believe that the secret lies in what your foot is doing. This kind of coordination is difficult at first but perseverance will greatly improve your internal clock.

Begin *without a metronome* by tapping your foot three times per beat. Your foot is now tapping the 1/8th note pulse. In the previous example each note will fall directly *between* your foot taps: so if you count "one and two and three and" as your foot goes *down up down up down up* you should be playing a note every time your foot is in the 'up' position and you are saying the word "and" out loud.

As this starts to become natural, try setting your metronome to 150 bpm (beats per minute) and hear the click as the 1/8th notes you have been tapping. Repeat the previous paragraph but with the metronome ticking.

Now set your metronome to 50bpm and keep your foot tapping three 1/8th notes per click (just as you were before). Repeat the previous exercise.

Finally, try to play this lick along with backing track one.

As your ears and internal clock start to process this advanced use of time and rhythmic placement your phrasing *will* start to feel more natural. This is one of those 'brick wall' exercises which when students start to grasp, their musical ability improves dramatically. Don't forget, this kind of placement can be applied to *any* musical style. You will see huge benefits in all your musical endeavours, and your perception of rhythmic time and space *within* the beat will increase dramatically.

The problem with any 'brick wall' exercise like this is that we can only knock out a few bricks at a time and sometimes it will feel like the mortar isn't even crumbling. The secret is to keep returning to the wall regularly and slowly and steadily working away at it.

These kinds of exercises feel uncomfortable, but that is good news: - by working outside of our comfort zones we know that we are practicing in the most beneficial way. We feel uncomfortable because our brain is working so hard to process the mental, spatial and physical aspects of our playing. Take a lot of breaks because much of the processing that the brain does is done in the 'down time' away from the guitar. Ten-minute bursts work great here.

Another 'Big Picture' Observation

The exercises in this chapter aren't just here to teach you a specific kind of rhythmic displacement. The big picture is that you are learning to begin at *any* point in the bar with *any* rhythmic value. These exercises may seem academic and cerebral right now; however very soon you should forget about specific displacements and just play. I promise that you will soon find you have developed the ability to consistently play *when* and *where* you like in the bar.

This kind of rhythmic freedom is one of the ultimate goals in music. If we are to be truly expressive in our playing an ability to put a note *anywhere* is surely an essential ability.

These are the exercises that 'opened up the beat' for me. The students that practice them diligently are the ones who quickly reach a whole other level of musical expression.

Isn't that better than using your practice time to simply run scales?

Let's continue with the displacement of the previous lick across the bar. When the beginning of the line falls on the 1/8th note you will find it easy, but when it falls on the 1/16th note it will be more difficult.

Example 3v:

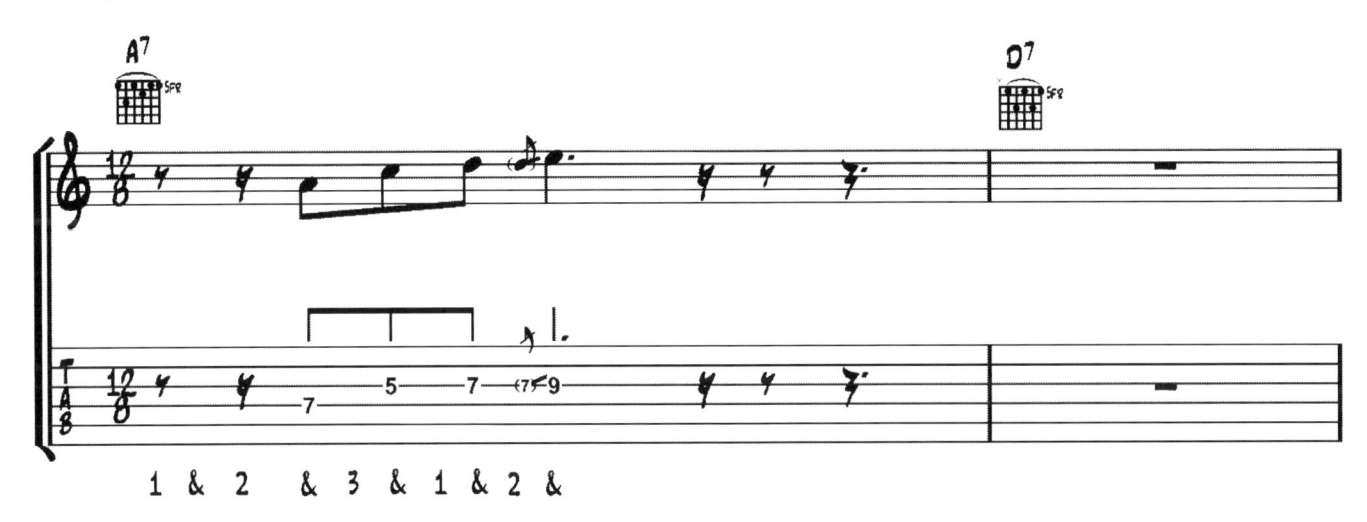

Continue with this 1/16th note displacement in the same way as you have in previous examples. Pay careful attention to beats three and four when the lick will start to cross the bar line as some very interesting results start to occur.

Repeat this kind of 1/16th note displacement with other licks that begin with 1/8th notes.

One of the main uses of all these displacements is to make greater use of single guitar licks. By disguising our vocabulary, playing them over different chord changes and starting the lick on different subdivisions of the beat, we can create thousands of subtle variations on a theme which all sound unique and fresh to the listener. We can cover great melodic ground with just a few simple licks.

Remember: *it's better to learn to play one lick in one hundred different ways than it is to learn one hundred different licks.*

This level of rhythmic perception frees us from regurgitating and 'chasing' licks around the fretboard, we can now create and genuinely improvise our solos with an individual freedom not available to pure 'lick' players.

When you *do* learn a new lick you will be able to manipulate it in many different ways to disguise its origin and make it unique to you.

A final thing to explore is the effect of displacement over more harmonically dense passages of music. When the chords are changing more quickly, displacement of a melodic phrase can be much more effective as you will continually be placing different notes from a lick over different chords in the harmony/rhythm guitar part.

The last four bars of the blues are a great way to practice this idea:

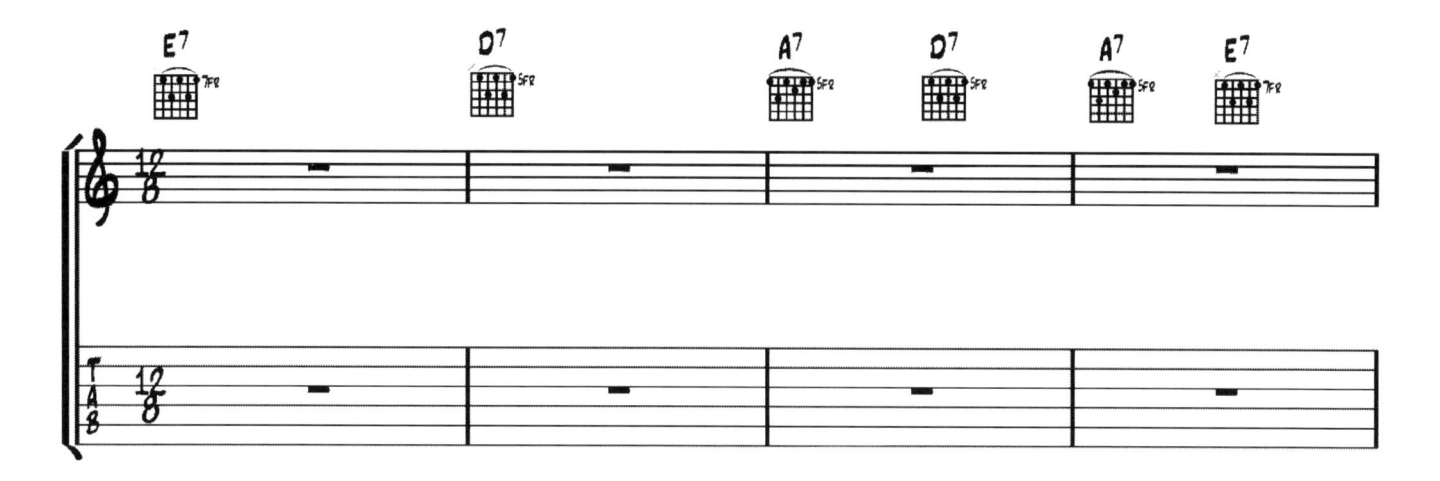

Take simple phrases and practice displacing them so that they cross the bar lines at different points. You will be amazed at how different your licks can sound.

This sort of practice is fantastic ear training because when you create new sounds that you like, you will unconsciously remember them and eventually they will flow freely when you improvise 'for real' at the gig.

Chapter 4: Developing Lines and Creativity

The concepts in this chapter all centre around the concept of creativity and how we can reach deep within ourselves to develop a personal and individual style. These exercises transcend genre and can be applied to almost any style of music. There are no right or wrong answers in these lessons as this chapter is about developing your own unique voice.

Creativity with Question and Answer Structures

In the blues, great importance is placed on phrase structure and keeping a musical dialogue running between each successive line. The easiest way to explain this dialogue is by the phrase 'question and answer' or 'call and response'. In the early spiritual music I referenced in the introduction this is easy to hear. The first phrase is a *call* and sets up the *response*. This structure continues throughout the whole piece of music.

For a slightly more up to date and 'guitary' illustration listen to the guitar solo in Stevie Ray Vaughan's *Lenny*. The whole thing is packed with this call and response idea. Even though both the call and the response are both played on the same instrument there are definitely echoes of the early gospel blues phrasing structure. B.B. King is another great exponent of this idea.

Practicing call and response by yourself can be a little challenging so if you can work on the following ideas with a musician friend you might find them a little more beneficial.

In this first set of exercises I will give you a set lick as a question, and you will be providing an answering phrase.

Begin by getting very familiar with the following lick.

Example 4a:

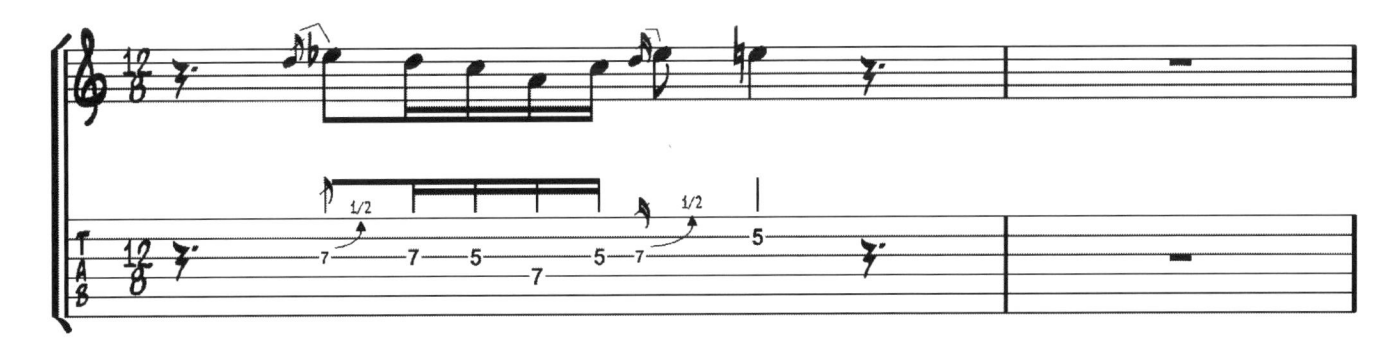

The line in the previous example is going to be your *question* phrase and will form a repeating figure throughout the 12 bar blues. Notice that it begins on beat two of the bar.

The first exercise is to play this lick in every alternate bar (bars one, three, five, etc.) and improvise your *own* answering phrase in the gaps in bars two, four, six, etc.

The 'scheme' of your solo will look like this:

60

The first exercise is to improvise *any* answering phrase you wish, with the only rule being that you *must* be ready to play the question phrase when it reoccurs in the following bar.

Again, there are no wrong answers to this exercise. Here is one of the infinite number of possibilities that I came up with.

Example 4b:

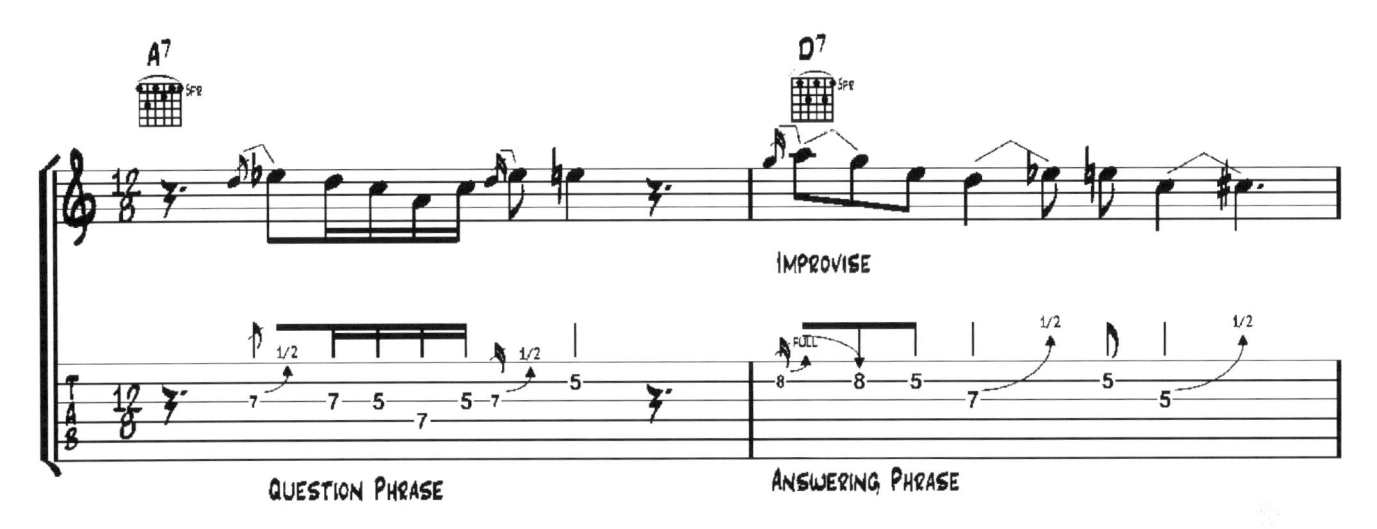

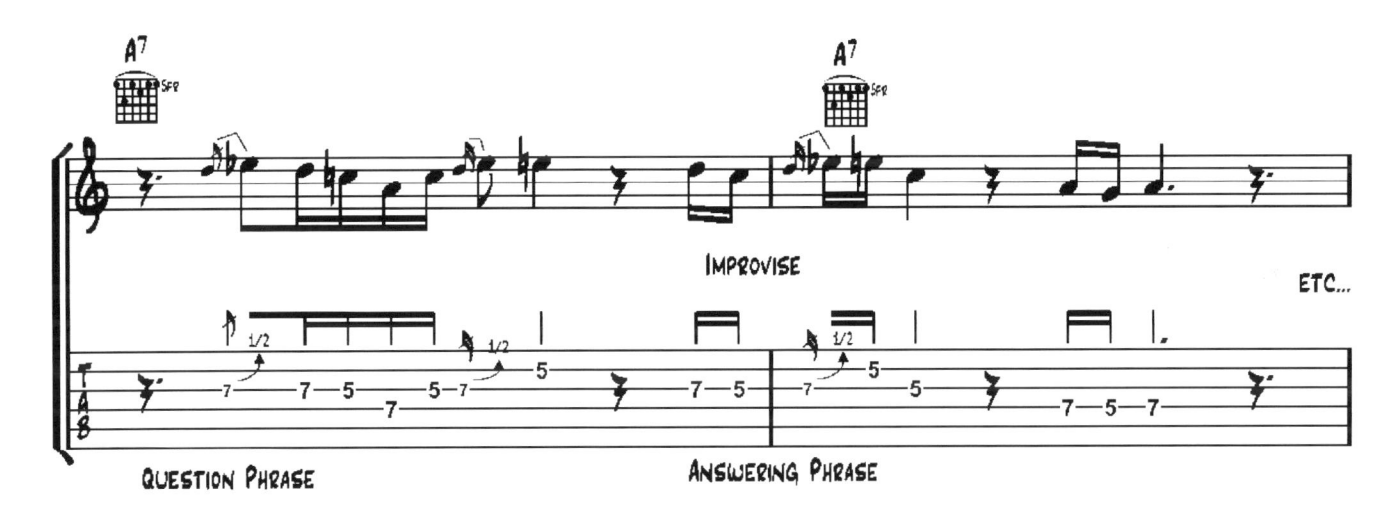

Try to play as many choruses of blues as you can, and find many answers to the exact same question phrase each time. By having to answer the same question in many different ways you will force yourself to become more creative in your answers. You will start to see your solo as one story full of connected ideas rather than just a series of short random ideas.

Even in this seemingly restrictive exercise I am still really giving you 'free rein' to fill in the answers as you please. You are simply being told to 'feel' what should come next, with very little in the way of limitations or structure.

In one sense, this is good because it will help you develop your own voice on the guitar, however in another sense, playing this freely is a little limited as a learning exercise because I'm not forcing you to play too far outside of your comfort zone.

In my life I have been fortunate enough to have some exceptional guitar teachers, and one sentence from Shaun Baxter has always stuck with me:
"It's a paradox; but the more you limit yourself, the more creative you are forced to become".

An analogy could be that if I sat you in a restaurant, you're not going to have to think too much about how to find food, but if I dropped you in a desert you would have to get pretty creative about finding your next meal. You may even do things that you never thought you were capable of to find sustenance.

With exercises designed to enhance creativity I firmly believe that if we are to find new ways to play our notes we have to isolate one very small creative aspect at a time and try to exhaust its possibilities before we move on.

Creativity by Limiting Rhythm

Let's look at some ways we can force ourselves to play something *new* within the above question and answer structure.

The first thing we can try is to create our answer with *exactly* the same rhythm as the question. This requires strict discipline and will quickly show us when our fingers, not our ears, try to take control of the guitar.

Here is just one example of using the same rhythm in the answering phrase.

Example 4c:

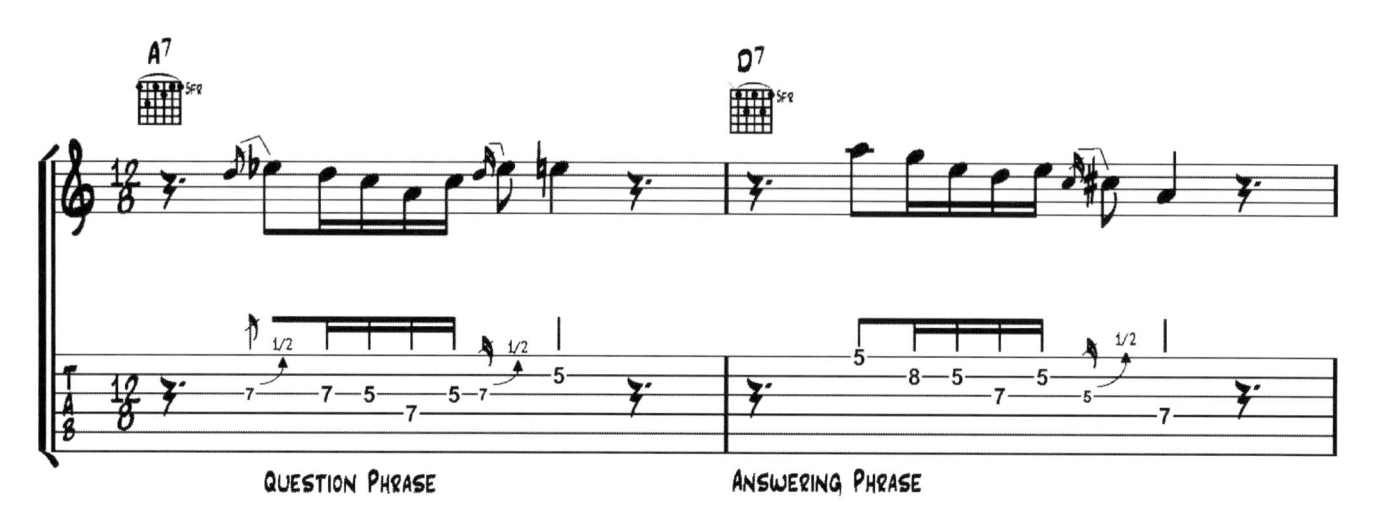

Obviously this is just one possible answering phrase, but I encourage you to play through many choruses of the blues and stick to answering the question with exactly the same rhythm, but with many different melodies.

Next, how about using the same rhythm for your answer but displacing it earlier or later by one or more 1/18th notes?

This example shows an answer that is one 1/8th note early.

Example 4d:

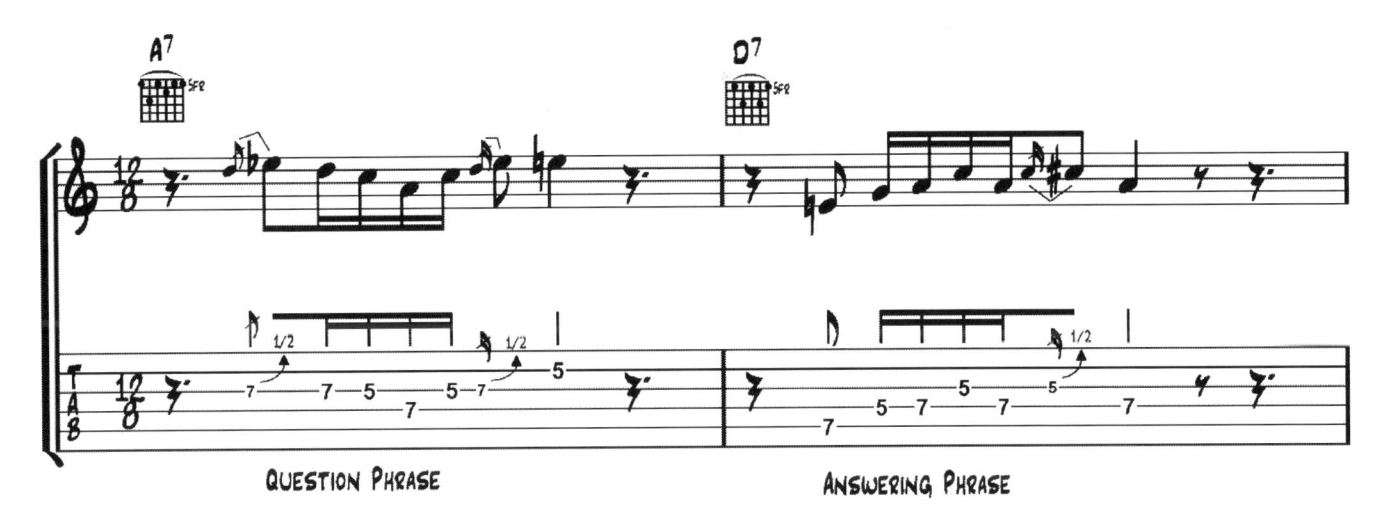

Here is just one example where we use the same rhythm starting one 1/8th note later.

Example 4e:

As you can see, the rhythm is identical but it starts one 1/8th note later and uses different notes.

Try to see if you can find ten different answering phrases beginning on beat two, then ten beginning one 1/8th note early, and finally ten beginning one 1/8th note late. This is difficult, but the idea is to *force* you to come up with new music on the spot. These exercises do get easier over time.

When you feel you have exhausted all your possibilities try beginning your answering phrase two 1/8ths earlier or later while still sticking to the same rhythm.

If I was to write out even just a few possible answers here for each displacement I would fill the book so it's up to you to get creative.

Do you remember how displacing a lick in chapter three completely altered the phrase's meaning and the melodic line that you were inspired to play after it? When you get tired of the previous exercises, try moving the question phrase an 1/8th note early or late and see how this affect your answer.

Example 4f: (Early)

Example 4g: (Late)

You have been locked into this rhythmic format for a while so now try allowing yourself to *freely* improvise an answer to the set question. You don't have to worry about keeping the same rhythm; just see what comes out.

After a few days of this kind of playing you will find that you're playing ideas spontaneously that you would never have thought possible.

Each day improvise a new melodic question and see how many ways you can find to answer it.

Working with another musician, ask them to give you a completely different question every two bars and work on improvising answers.

Creativity by Limiting Range

Sticking to just one rhythm is not the only way to get creative when we're improvising. How about simply limiting the musical *range* that we use when we solo?

In the following exercise you are only allowed to use these four notes in your answer:

Begin by brain-storming all the possible techniques you can imagine to make these notes come alive.

My list includes, but is not limited to:

Rhythm

Play fast (high density of notes)
Play slow (low density of notes)

Short burst of fast notes surrounded by long rests
Long bursts of fast notes surrounded by rests

Stick to one rhythm and alter the melody
Stick to one sequence of notes and alter the rhythm

Play duplets or 4 against 3 feel

Play different rhythms on one note.
Play different rhythms on one note while gradually bending it.

Beginning and Ending Notes

Sliding into notes (beginning and during phrases)
Sliding out of notes (after and during phrases)

Slide in/out slowly, slide in quickly, slide from below, slide from above

Slide to an open string
Slide up and off the neck very quickly
Wide Vibrato
Narrow Vibrato
Narrow Vibrato *becoming* wide vibrato and vice versa
Vibrato before sliding out of a phrase

Go to appendix B for vibrato technique exercises.

Bending

Focus on semitone bends
Focus on tone bends
Focus on one-and-a-half tone bends
Bend *very* slowly
Bend quickly
See how many 'in between' (microtone) notes you can find by bending very gradually from one note to another
Repeatedly pick slowly during a bend
Repeatedly pick quickly during a bend
Pre-bend - bend the note to pitch *before* picking it and then release
Bend a note up but don't release the pitch
Bend a note up but 'kill' it with the picking hand
Bend a note up and then release the bend quickly / slowly
Bend repeatedly from one pitch to another
Double-stop bends (bend two notes simultaneously)

Check out appendix A for more information on bending technique.

Duration/Frequency

Play for one beat
Play for two beats
Etc.

Play only one note
Play only two notes
Etc

Play long full notes
Play short staccato notes

Only play on beat one/two etc.

Pick Angle

Angle the pick sharply against the strings
Angle the pick flat against the strings
Change the pick angle *during* the phrase

Alter Picking Dynamics (more on this later)

Pick every note
Pick hard
Pick soft

Pick near the bridge
Pick near the neck
Move pick from the bridge towards the deck *during* the phrase

Get louder / quieter during a phrase

Articulation

Play legato
Pick everything
Only use Hammer-Ons and Pull-Offs

Pick the first note of a phrase and play the rest legato (Hammer-ons and Pull-offs)
Pick the first two notes of a phrase and play the rest legato.
Etc.

Play double stops (two notes at the same time)

Add as many ideas as you can to these lists.

While I feel slightly guilty for simply listing ideas for you to experiment with, I feel there is significant benefit to be had here by picking just one of these concepts each day and seeing how much mileage you can gain from it.

Take your chosen idea and stick to *only* the four notes given above - try to find as many ways as you can to apply that idea musically. This *is* difficult at first but if you stick with it you will force yourself to be creative within the confines of the exercise.

You *will* find new ways to approach your melodic soloing if you do it for long enough and these ideas will easily transfer themselves to the full licks and lines that you already know.

Finally, make sure you do apply these ideas *musically*. Instead of limiting your note range, play whole solos focusing on just one or two of the listed approaches. By using these ideas in a realistic context you will internalise them and they will quickly become an integral part of your playing.

Remember our premise: We all have the same 12 notes. It is *how* and *when* we play them that set us apart from one another. It is easy to hear the players who have worked on expressive exercises like this and the ones who haven't.

Exercises that focus on creativity are always by definition going to be a little bit "out there", and I certainly don't want to get too existential here; but the more you put into practicing these ideas, the deeper you will look inside yourself and the more personal your sound will become.

After a while, your 'borrowed' licks won't sound borrowed: You'll be playing them in your own way.

Do you want to be unique and instantly recognisable or do you want to be just another clone?

Asking the Question

We previously took a detailed look at *answering* a set musical question with an improvised phrase. This is a great exercise and helps you to dig deep within yourself rhythmically, melodically and expressively.

However, advanced musicians are often thinking ahead about phrases that are yet to be played. It is not uncommon to be thinking at least two phrases ahead and to have a kind of planned 'outline' or 'scheme' for the solo.

This may be hard to comprehend at first, but it *is* possible to learn to project what you'll be doing a couple of bars in the future. Rather than thinking of this like a complex game of chess, imagine yourself as an artist who is making a very early, rough sketch of the location of objects in a landscape painting. Things may move around later and there may be no detail yet, but there is definitely an overarching scheme of where they want to take the picture.

The difficult part is how to get away from the *now* and to start conceptualising the *then*. We need to learn to think ahead.

The best exercise I have seen to encourage this kind of musical forethought it to reverse the previous question and answer exercise. We will work with a set answering phrase but try to create as many ways as we can to set it up with an original question. By doing this we are forced to imagine/hear in our head the phrase that is going to come after our next line and thus develop our forward-thinking ability.

Learn the following lick:

Example 4h:

This will be our answering phrase throughout the next section. Look at the following soloing scheme. It is the reverse of the one on page 60.

As you can see, your job is to set up the answering lick by spontaneously improvising a new question in bars one, three and five etc.

This is actually much harder than you may think, especially when you consider that the answer should always be relevant and in some way musically linked to the question.

Some good advice is to try to keep the rhythm and placement of the answering phrase in your head just before and during your question phrase. If you're very conscious of where you're going you might find it easier to 'blend' your question and answer into one cohesive musical statement.

Another idea is to not be too strict about the *placement* of the answering phrase. While I believe you should keep the answering phrase as it is, if you feel you should play it a bit earlier or later, go ahead.

This kind of freedom is helpful to get you into the exercise, but when you're more confident try to force yourself to always keep the answering lick in the predefined place as above. In this case it's on beat two. The following example shows just a couple of ways that I approached the exercise.

Example 4i:

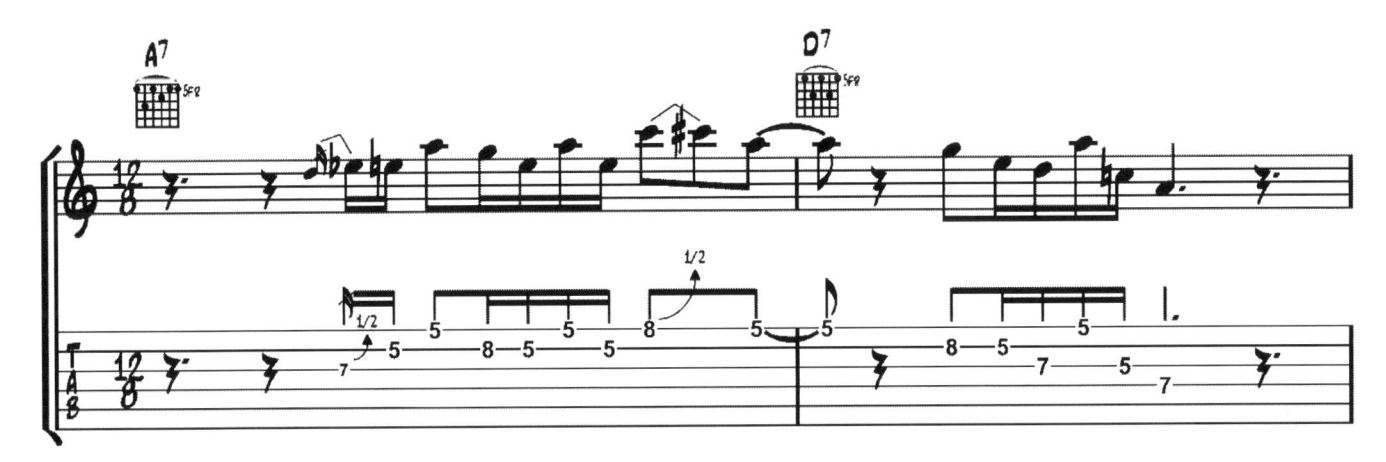

Example 4j:

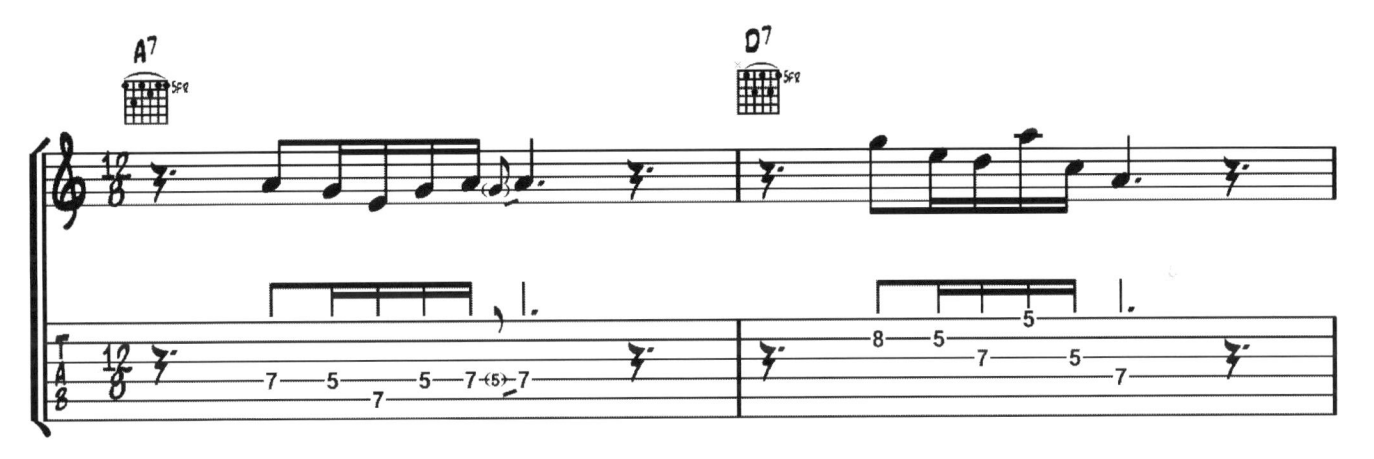

Example 4k:

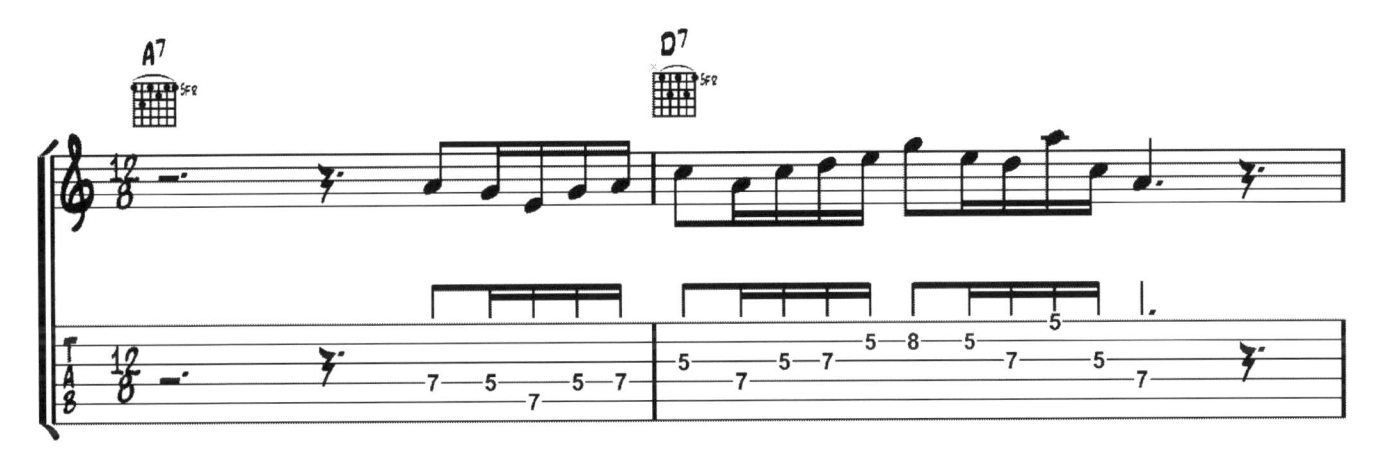

In exercise 4i, my approach was to try to create two rhythmically distinct yet symbiotic phrases that functioned as the 'traditional' question and answer phrasing structure. Notice that my question phrase tends to ascend in pitch while my answer generally descends. This is common and a good starting point on which to model your practice.

Exercise 4j is slightly different; I purposely use the rhythmic structure of my answering phrase in my question. This approach will normally develop a strong link between the question and answer licks.

Finally in exercise 4k I take a different approach and 'blend' my question phrase into the answer using a short rhythmic sequence. I personally find this idea much harder to work on, but it does quickly give great benefits.

Come up with your own answering phrases and try to do this exercise every day. Remember, the overall goal is to be able to think about and hear the line you will be playing *after* the one you are playing now. This kind of forward thinking helps you strongly structure your solo and take your audience on a journey by developing a melodic 'thread' or pathway throughout your whole improvisation.

Developing a Melodic Line

The following rhythmic exercise is one of my favourites to give to students who struggle to develop a melodic idea throughout a whole solo. This exercise requires quite a lot of concentration in your practice time, but you will quickly notice an improvement in your ability to naturally build a strong melodic thread throughout your improvisation.

The exercise sounds simple on paper but in actual fact it takes a lot of discipline and patience to master.

1) Take a short, fixed rhythm and use it to improvise a melodic line
2) Repeat the rhythm once per bar for three bars, varying the melody each time
3) In the fourth bar, play the rhythm again however this time freely develop the rhythm
4) Use the rhythm you created at the end of bar four as the set rhythm for the next four bars
5) Repeat

The secret to making this exercise work is to keep the rhythms short and uncomplicated at first. I think this kind of exercise is much easier to see musically than it is to explain in words. Take a look at example 4l.

Example 4l:

I begin with a *very* simple phrase; just a couple of notes and repeat that exact same rhythm for the first three bars. In bar four I trust my ear and allow myself to develop the idea very slightly. A small variation is much better than a full bar of improvisation here.

The tricky bit is to *remember the last couple of notes you played in bar four*. Take the *rhythm* of the notes in bar 4 and base a short phrase around that rhythm in bar five. Once you have your new, developed rhythm stick with it and repeat the process.

Compare bar 12 to bar 1. These lines are very different but we have arrived at the complexity in bar 12 through a natural, *organic* process.

For a really masterful demonstration of this kind of rhythmic development, one of the best pieces of music you can listen to is the first movement of **Beethoven's Fifth Symphony in C Minor.**

While not strictly the blues, you can easily hear how he develops a four note phrase into one of the most important pieces of music ever written. Listen to how the phrase develops rhythmically throughout the piece and changes with subtle and not-so-subtle use of orchestration and dynamics. It's the perfect lesson in creating something massive out of the smallest of rhythmic fragments.

While it isn't as explicit as Beethoven's Fifth, a bluesier example of all the techniques in this chapter, including the rhythmic development ideas in this section is **Lucille by B.B. King**.

There's an extremely strong question and answer theme running throughout the song, especially in the longer solos, but if you listen attentively you can clearly hear how he rhythmically develops his melody from one phrase to the next.

Many people will turn around to me at this point and say, "yes, but he just feels it, he probably never even thought about it like this".

I'm sure those people are right, however if we are to learn to develop as musicians, we often need to break down the 'unconscious' skills of talented musicians into tangible, learnable chunks and work on them as exercises before they eventually become 'I'm just feeling it' to us too.

Imagine you were going to learn a magic trick from an illusionist. They would be an inadequate teacher if they just said "it's magic!"

The previous example revolves around your *awareness* as a player, not just rhythmic development.
You have to be in control of what you're playing for it to work and you need to consciously remember the previous rhythm you played. It's a fantastic exercise to move away from just 'noodling' on the guitar and working towards actually being in control of what you play.

Tonal Variation with Phrasing

On page 65 I quickly gave you some ideas about how to vary the sound of your playing by varying the angle of your pick. I think this is one of the most criminally overlooked areas of guitar playing and not enough attention is given to the thousands of subtle variations you can give to a phrase just by simply using your plectrum.

"If you go to see a professional orchestra, it is possible that the lead violinist is playing a £1,200,000 Stradivarius. The bow, just the stick and horse hair they are using can cost upwards of £60,000.

As guitarists, we use a 50p piece of plastic.

Virtually every single tone you create on the guitar starts with the pick, so it follows that we have a lot of work to do to get as much good tone out of our plectrum as possible."

- Taken from **Complete Technique for Modern Guitar**

Here's a simple demonstration. Compare these two identical lines. The first is played with a pick held lightly at a normal angle; the second is played *hard and aggressively* with the pick angled almost at 90 degrees to the strings.

They are both played with the plectrum located between the neck and the middle pickup and both examples are played with the same amp settings and pickup selection.

Example 4m:

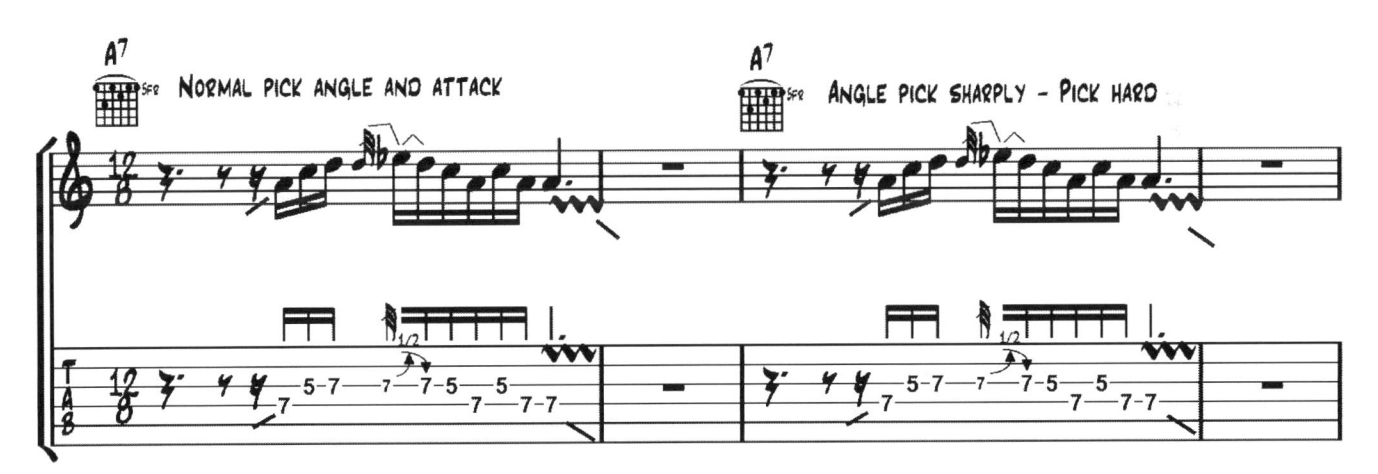

There is a dramatic difference between the two lines with a couple of noticeable things happening.

Even forgetting the pick angle for a second, when you pick harder, you send more of the guitar signal to the amp. This will result in the ability to use less gain to achieve an over driven tone. This is how you generate that clean, slightly broken up sound that is perfect for blues.

I would never say pick hard *all* the time, but in general I find that most guitarists don't practice picking hard on a regular basis. So much is (quite rightly) written about finding a consistent, even picking technique that colour and tonal possibilities are often forgotten.

Try picking really hard in a few practice sessions; really overdo it. You might find that you're not able to play some of the licks that you thought you knew: relearn them but with this time use much harder picking.

By just relearning a few of your licks in this way you will find it much easier to access all the tonal colours and possibilities that can be achieved by simply playing harder.

The following is a simple exercise to help you learn to manage your picking attack. Begin by playing softly and see how many different volumes you can find between 'quiet' and 'loud'.

Example 4n:

If you're using a decent amplifier then you should be able to set it so that when you play softly your sound is clean, but when you start to increase the power of your attack the sound starts to break up and distort.

As I'm sure you can imagine, the tonal possibilities are immense.

One of the things you will also find is that when you play with different picking dynamics in this way, is that you will actually start to phrase your lines slightly differently. You will end up altering rhythms and 'accidentally' finding new ways to phrase your lines.

Try playing a few licks with the picking approach shown in example 4n. Gradually pick harder throughout the lick. Try picking hard to begin with and gradually get softer. You could play the whole lick quietly and accentuate a couple of notes or play loudly and leave some 'holes' in the lick when you pick very lightly.

Pick Angle and Phrasing

As you heard in example 4m, the angle at which you strike the strings with the plectrum has a huge effect on your tone (and phrasing) too.

Normally we hold the plectrum at a very slight angle to the strings to help the curved edge 'roll' through the string and create a consistent tone. When we start to angle the pick more sharply to the string a few things start to happen.

First of all, the tone of our guitar dramatically changes, but it also becomes much harder to physically move the plectrum through the strings to create a note.

You might find that because it is more difficult to push the pick through the strings, the note you create is very slightly delayed from when you were expecting to hear it.

In essence we have started to play slightly behind the beat. I'll admit, it's not necessarily the most controlled way to practice the important skill of behind-the-beat playing but it can be a great way to access this difficult rhythmic technique fairly easily.

Compare the two lines:

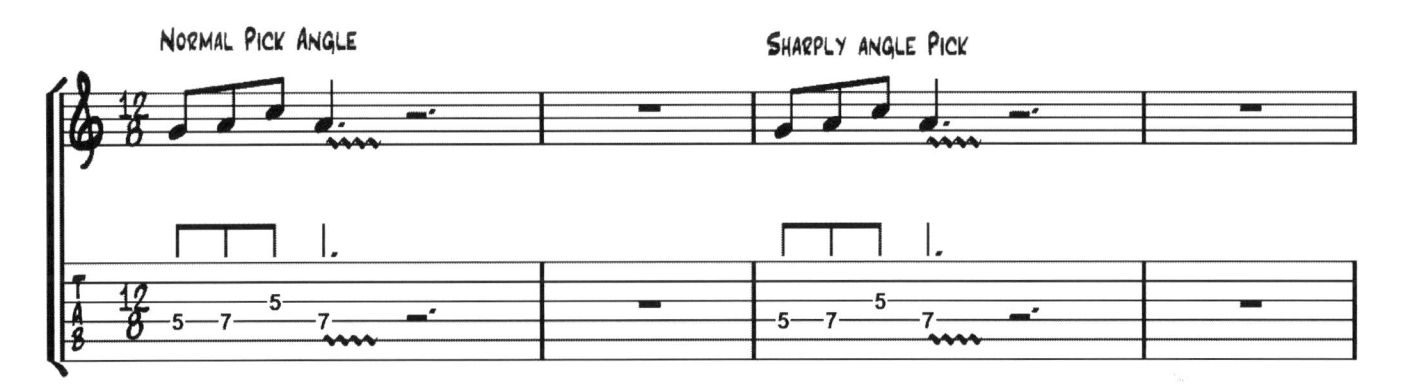

Example 4o:

Notice that not only has the tone changed considerably, the notes in the second line have started to fall very slightly behind the beat.

Behind-the-beat playing is an extremely desirable skill and this method of angling the pick is a great way to 'fake it until you make it'. This is *not* the way to build a consistent, controllable behind-the-beat feel, but if you change the angle of your pick during a melodic line you will start to create some very interesting phrasing variations.

Practice changing your pick angle throughout a guitar lick that you know extremely well. Listen to the way the following lick pushes and pulls against the beat as I vary my pick angle.

Example 4p:

An equally effective way to alter your tone is to pick near the bridge, near the neck or anywhere in-between.

Try playing the above lick with different pick placement. Playing near the bridge will give you a thin, harsh tone which will soften off as you move towards the neck. Try changing your pick position from forward to back (and vice versa) as you play a line.

We can combine any of the three techniques in this section:

Play Hard / Play Soft
Normal Pick Angle / Sharp Pick Angle
Pick Near the Bridge / Pick Near the Neck

This means that our right hand can be constantly evolving, fluidly changing between any of the permutations above. This kind of variance in attack from our picking hand creates a vocal, three dimensional aspect to our sound and continually changes our amplifier's reaction to our playing.

Suddenly our playing becomes more than just notes; there is a very human dynamic, full of nuance and personality. There are subtle textural differences in each and every note and our playing becomes personal and unique.

Time spent working on varying your picking approach will set you head and shoulders above the crowd.

Chapter 5: Range and Other Positions on the Neck

So far in this book we have concentrated on a very small range of notes in just one area of the guitar. - I can already imagine the negative reviews coming in on Amazon! However, as you know, I think that by sometimes limiting the amount of notes we allow ourselves to play, we can focus much more deeply on the *how* and the *when* of our phrasing, and not get bogged down in note choice. In this chapter we will look at how to expand our ideas all over the fretboard.

The great news is that if you have worked hard at the concepts in this book, it is very easy to apply these techniques to other areas of the neck. In fact, if you have really spent some time on these ideas you will have started to *internalise* these ideas on a deep musical level, so you won't even have to think about applying them to new scale shapes or licks anymore.

Most guitarists think about the guitar neck by breaking it up into chunks, or *positions.*

It is common to split the neck into five different positions of the same scale. Each position will have a different scale shape and we normally number these as 'shape one', 'shape two', 'shape three', etc.

The scale shape we have been using so far is A minor pentatonic shape one:

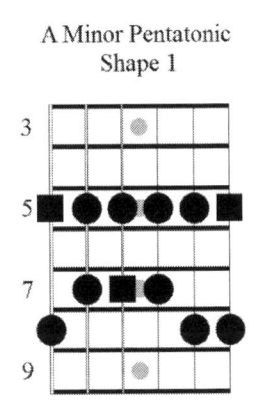

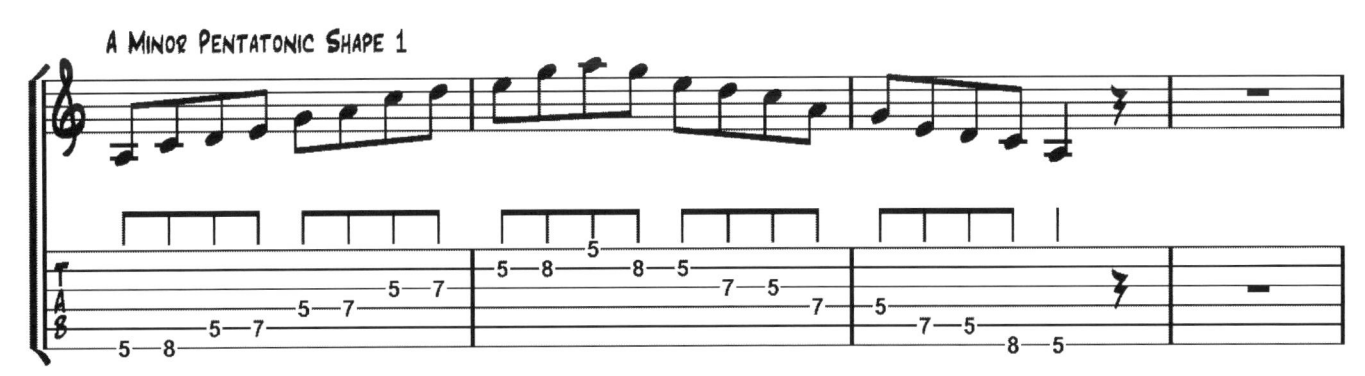

A Minor Pentatonic Shape 1

A MINOR PENTATONIC SHAPE 1

In this chapter we will explore the other four shapes of the A minor pentatonic scale, look at some useful vocabulary for each one, discuss their advantages and disadvantages and then finally look at how we can join them up to form runs that ascend and descend the entire neck.

A Minor Pentatonic Shape Two

Shape two is one of the most commonly used positions in which to solo. You may have heard of the phrase "The B.B. box", which refers to the notes on the top two or three strings of shape two. It is certainly true that B.B. King uses this position frequently in his playing and a lot of common blues phrases and vocabulary 'live' there.

Example 5a:

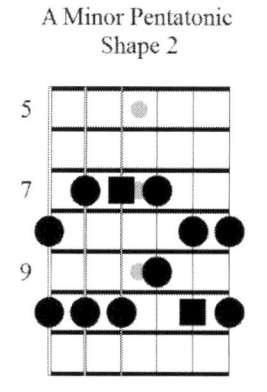

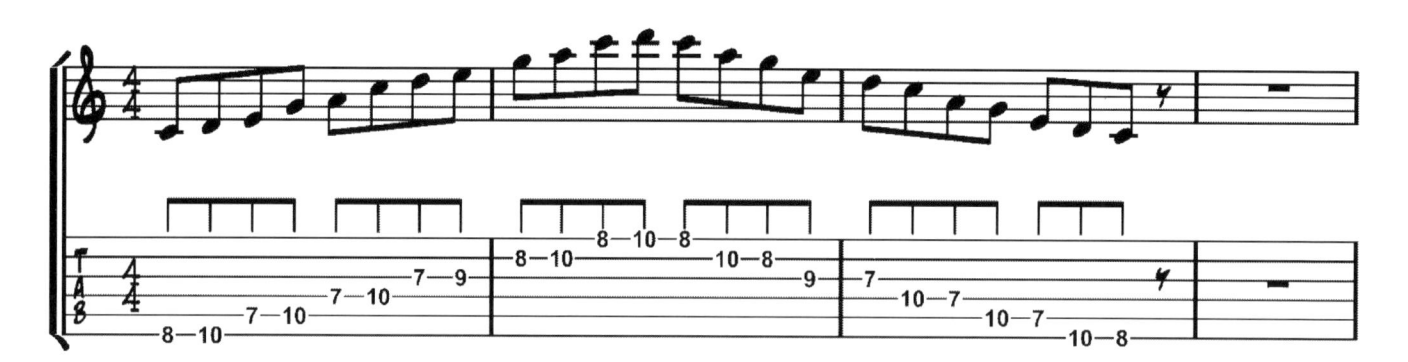

A Minor Pentatonic
Shape 2

```
-----------------8—10—8------------------------------
-------------8—10---------10—8----------------------
----------7—9----------------------9---7------------
------7—10----------------------------10—7---------
---7—10-------------------------------------10—7---
-8—10----------------------------------------10—8--
```

It is important you realise that with this kind of fretboard positional system, shape one will always interlock with shape two, which in turn will interlock with shape three, etc. You should be able to see this by comparing the higher notes on each string in shape one with the lower notes on each string in shape two. They fit together like a jigsaw.

Also notice that despite using a completely different fingering and scale shape, the majority of the pitches in shape two are identical to those in shape one. In fact, we have only managed to extend the range of the minor pentatonic scale by one tone on the top string. In other words, the top note of A minor pentatonic shape one is a C (8th fret) and the top note of A minor pentatonic shape two is a D (10th fret). It's good to remember this when we get obsessed with learning a scale all over the fretboard.

If we're going to be playing the same notes, and only extending the range of the scale by one tone, you may be asking what the point is in learning all these new shapes.

The answer is that different fingering patterns lend themselves to different licks, phrases and vocabulary.

The intervals of the pentatonic scale (root, b3, 4, 5, and b7) lie in different physical locations on the neck so it may be easier to bend or manipulate intervals that you may not have been comfortable doing in other shapes.

Tone is also a consideration.

When the same pitches fall on different strings their actual tone can be markedly different. For example, listen to the tone of a C note played on the 3rd string compared to the tone of the same C played on the 4th string.

Example 5b:

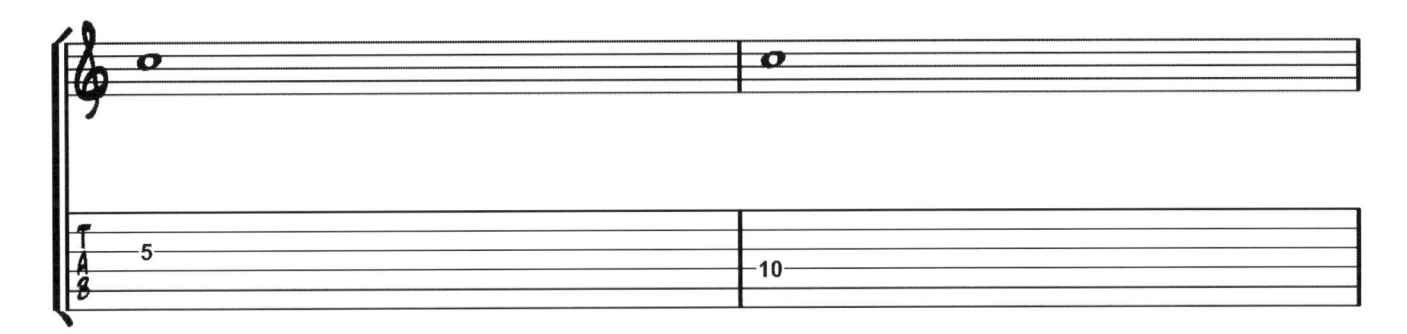

I'm sure you can hear the difference in tone here, however subtle it may be. This is one of the main reasons we use different shapes; an identical phrase will take on a different tone and phrasing when we use a different fingering pattern and play it on different strings. It is these kinds of subtleties that set us apart as individual players, which when combined with the rhythm and phrasing techniques in the previous chapters they can really help to create interesting, unique and idiomatic soloing.

Here are some of the kinds of short, typical phrases that often occur in shape two of the minor pentatonic scale.

Example 5c:

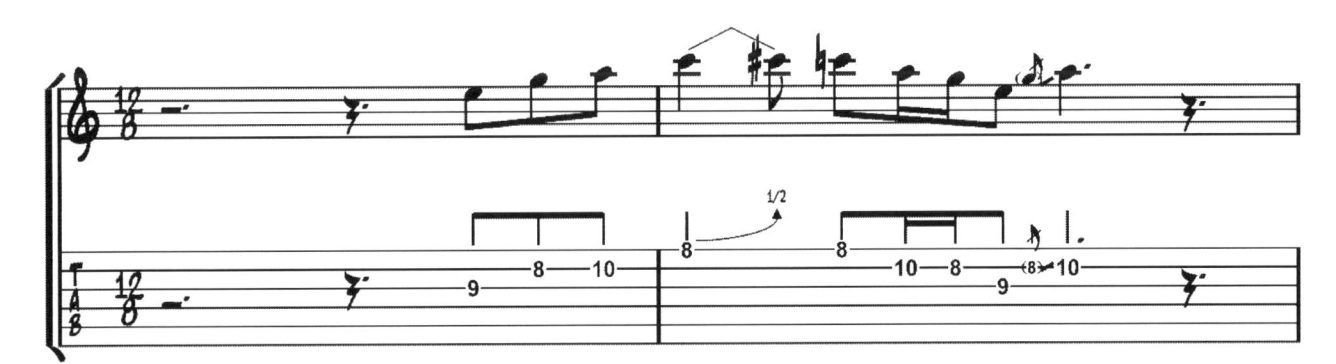

Example 5d:

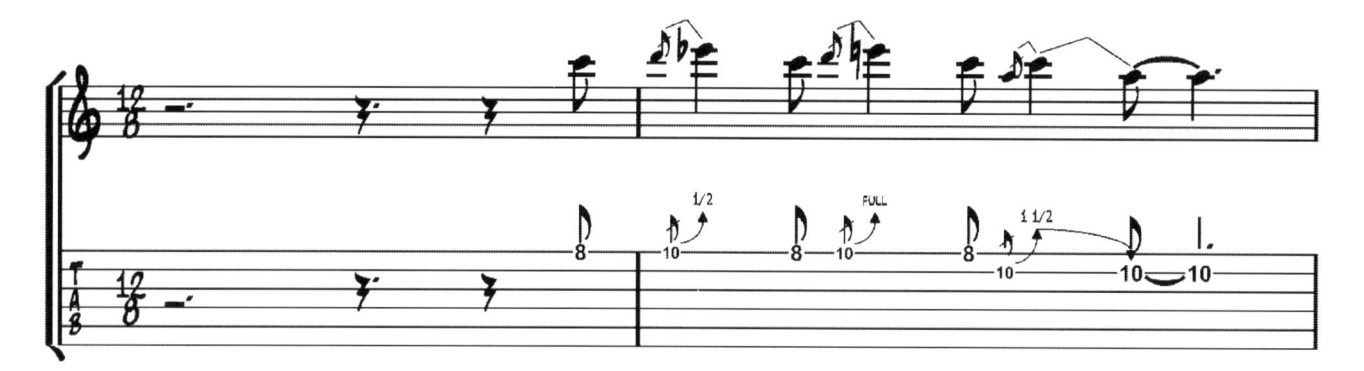

Example 5e:

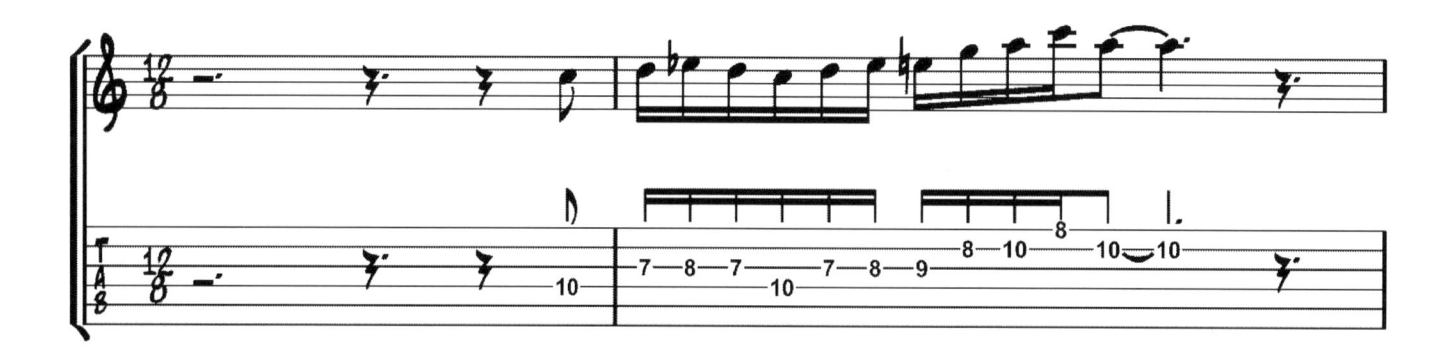

Example 5e uses the 'Blues Scale': This will be covered in more detail in The Complete Guide to Playing Blues Guitar Part Three.

Of course this is just a tiny sample but hopefully it's enough to get you into the idiomatic way that shape two can be used.

Pick some of your favourite phrasing ideas from earlier in the book and spend as much time as you can coming up with your own ideas in this new position.

Finally, if you want to get into using these shapes as quickly as possible, *transcribe* (steal!) ideas from your favourite players. If you use the phrasing techniques from this book, no one will ever know where these lines came from!

I mentioned earlier that shape one and shape two interlock. It is very common to change position from shape one to shape two using slides. Here are a few common ways to ascend from shape one into shape two.

Example 5f (a):

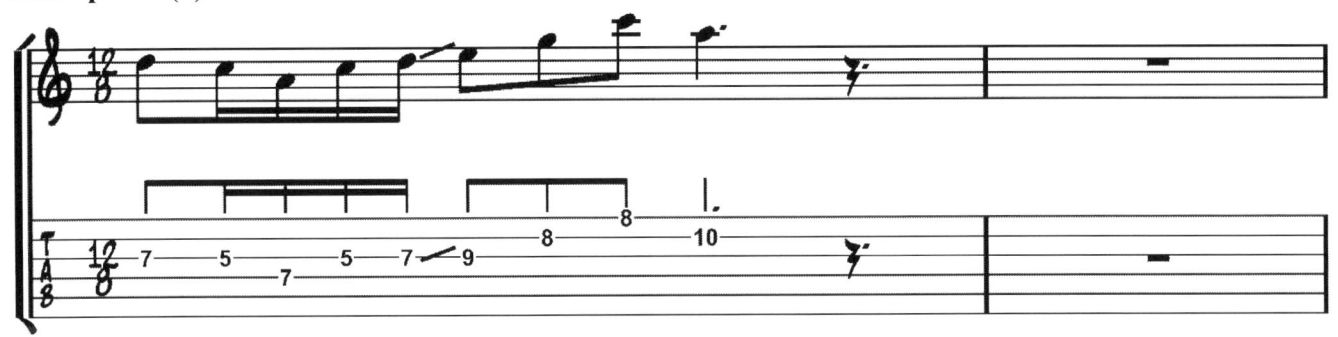

Example 5f (b):

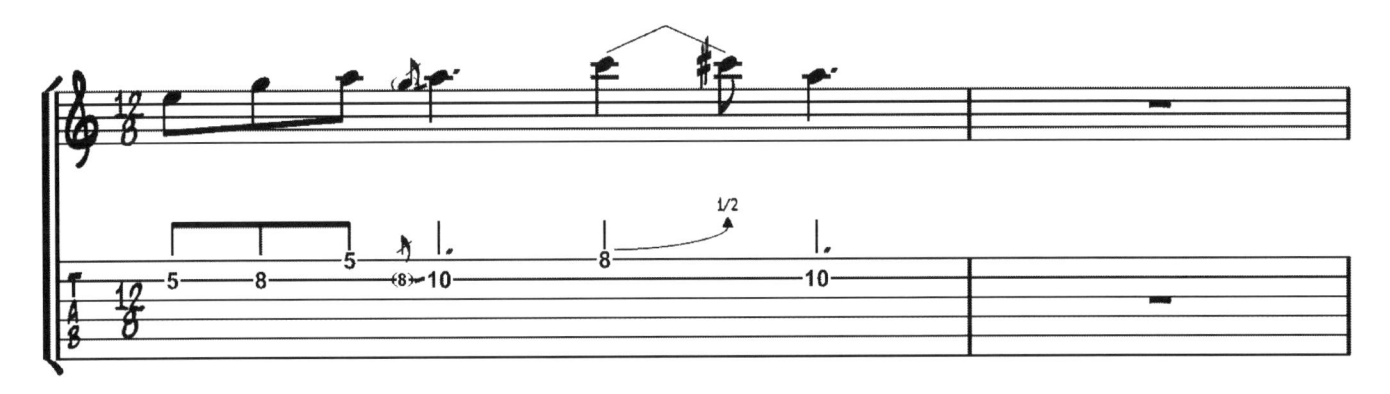

Example 5f (c):

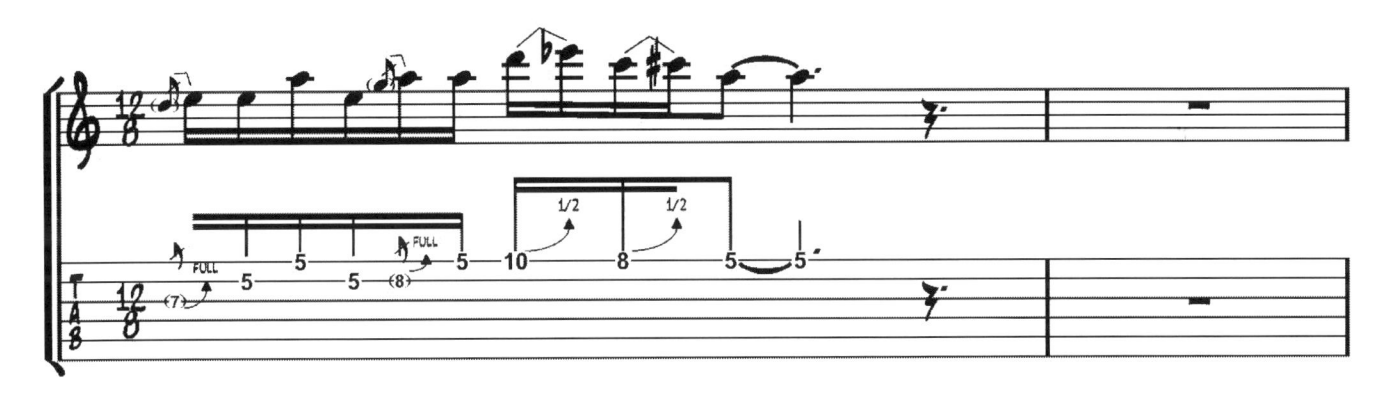

These are just a few ideas to get you going. See how many different melodic lines you can find while moving between the shapes.

It is important to practice these shapes in many other keys to get used to playing them in different areas on the guitar neck. Find some slow blues backing tracks and practice moving between shape one and two in different keys.

A Minor Pentatonic Shape Three

Shape three is one of my favourite pentatonic shapes to explore. I enjoy experimenting with the simple pattern on the bottom three strings and the opportunities for bending notes on the top three strings. If you're practicing ascending and descending this scale, use your first finger to play the lower note on each string and switch between your 3rd and 4th fingers to play the higher notes.

In my opinion, shape three is *slightly* less commonly used but don't let that put you off. The fingering pattern generates some wonderful and unique phrasing opportunities.

Example 5g:

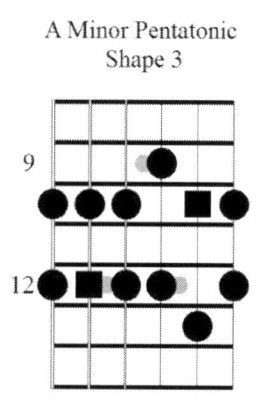

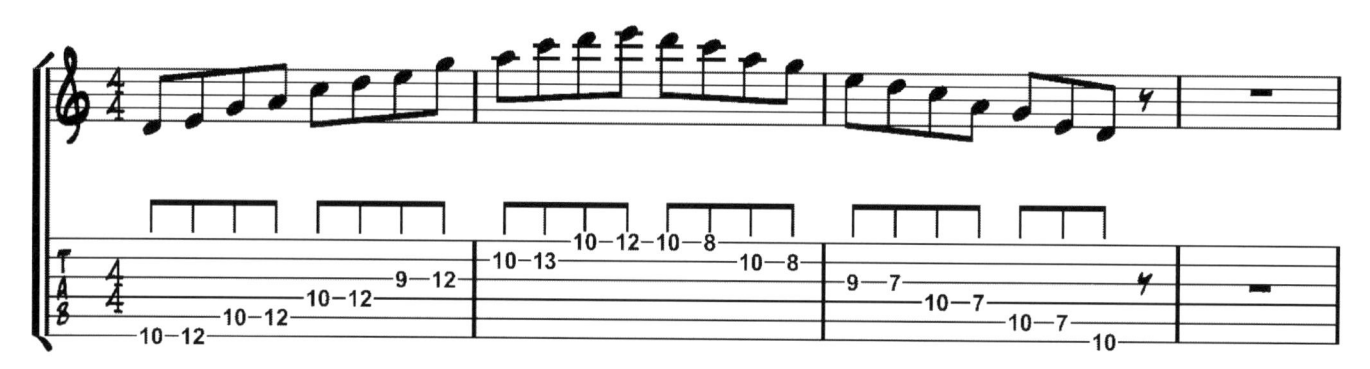

Once again, here are a few sample licks to help you quickly find some useful points of the scale shape to explore. Of course, you should also work to generate your own personal shape three licks and vocabulary by using the concepts in this book.

Example 5h:

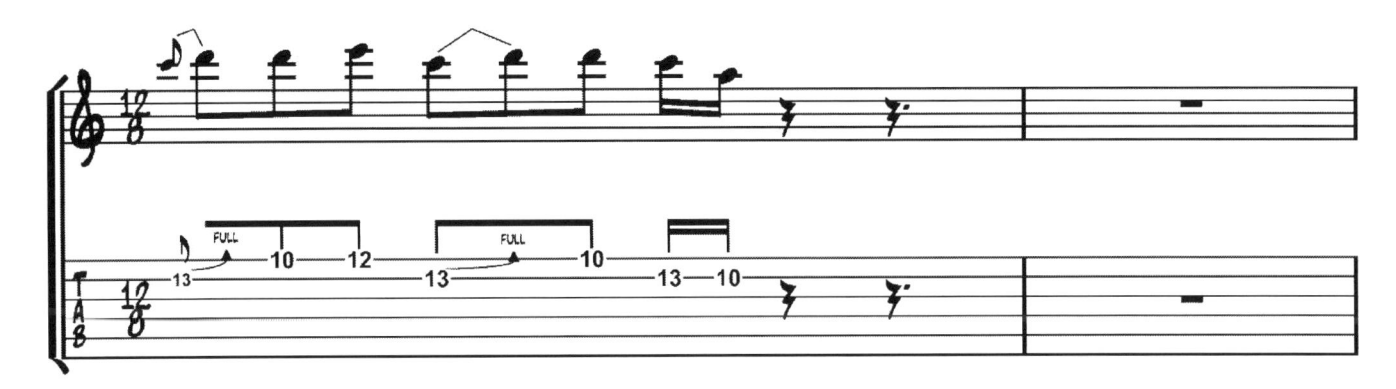

Example 5i:

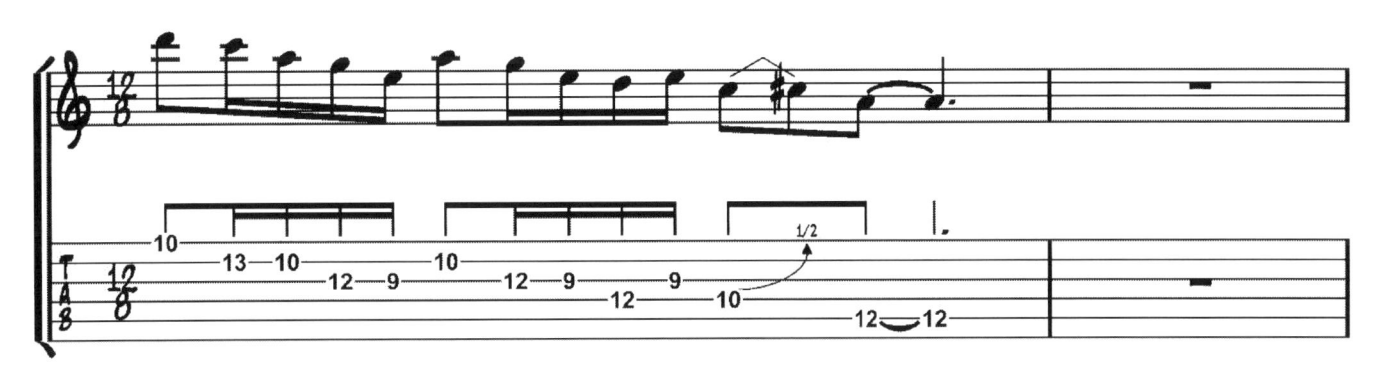

Example 5j:

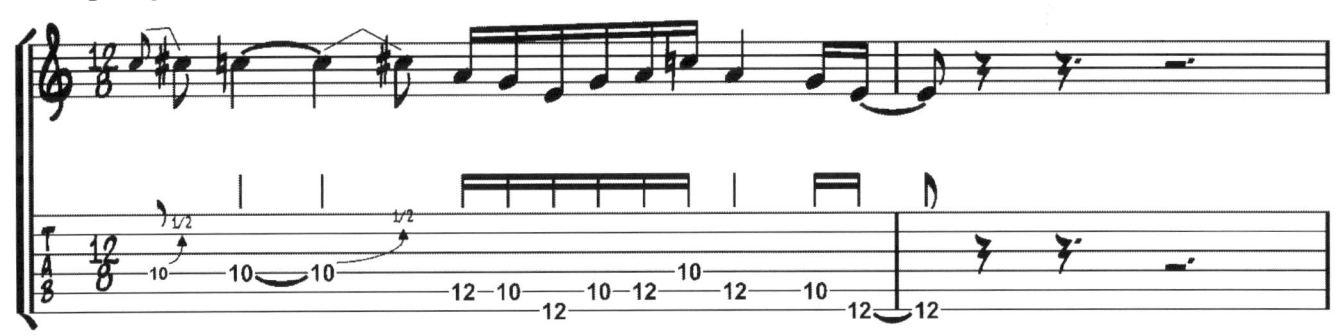

Try the following ideas to help you move seamlessly from position two into position three:

Example 5k (a):

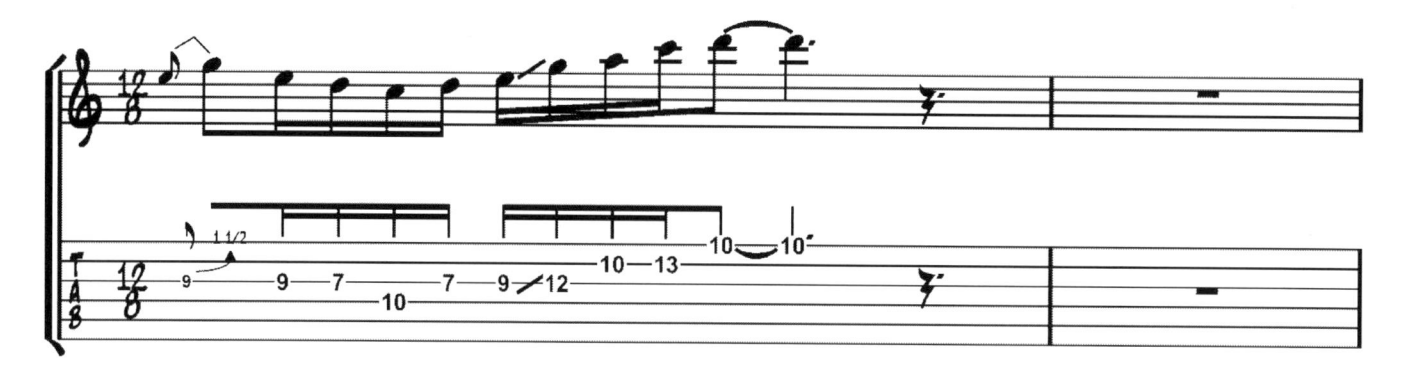

Example 5k (b):

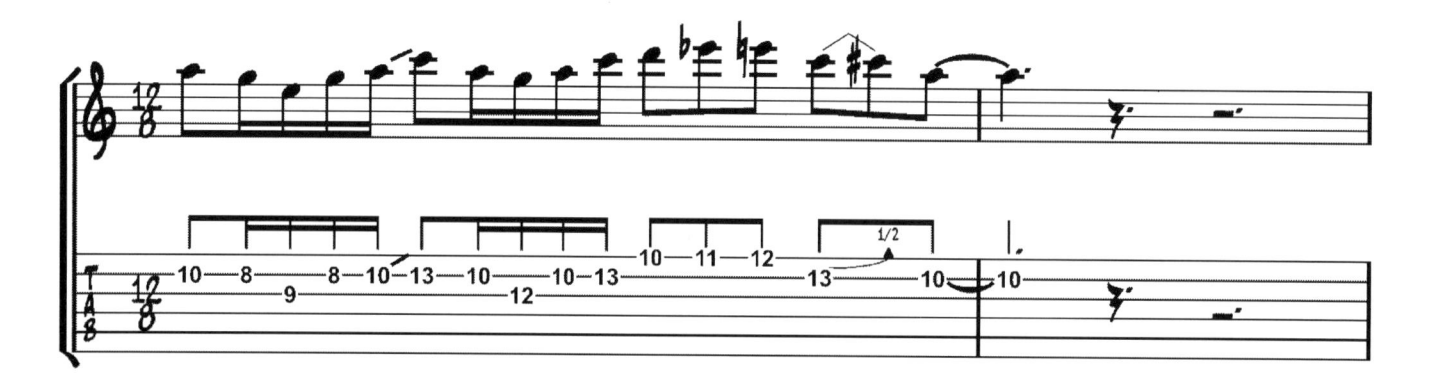

(Blues Scale)

Example 5k (c):

(Blues Scale)

Try linking up some connecting lines to move from shape one via shape two into shape three.

A Minor Pentatonic Shape Four

Shape four is one of the most commonly used positions of the minor pentatonic scale. It has many similarities with shape one but the slightly different pattern which is caused by the tuning idiosyncrasies of the guitar. Shape four gives us some great melodic opportunities. *Unison bends* in particular are common here.

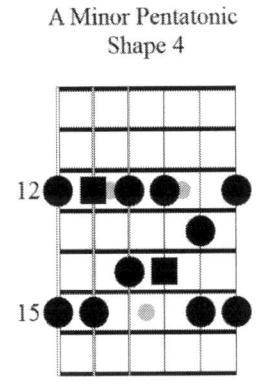

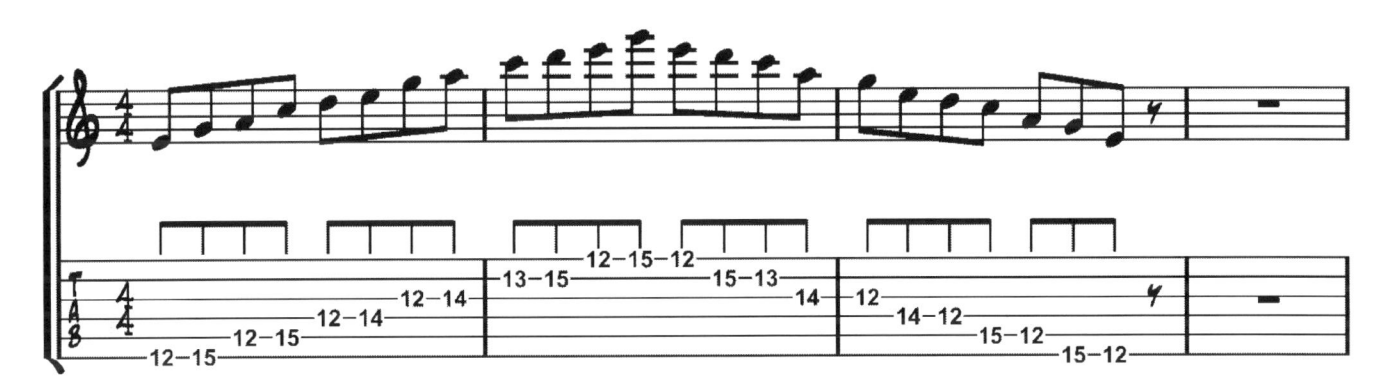

Example 5l:

Here are some useful licks based around shape four.

Example 5m:

Example 5n:

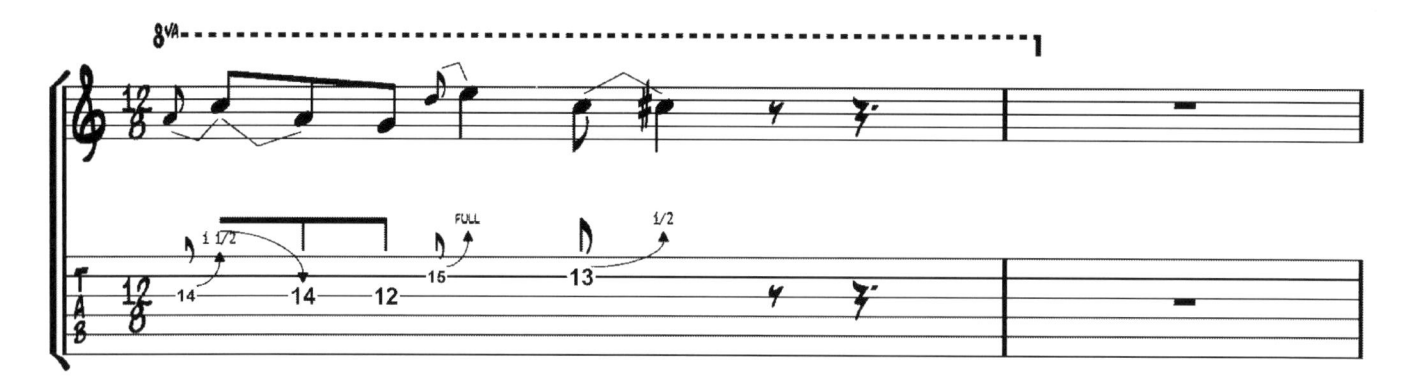

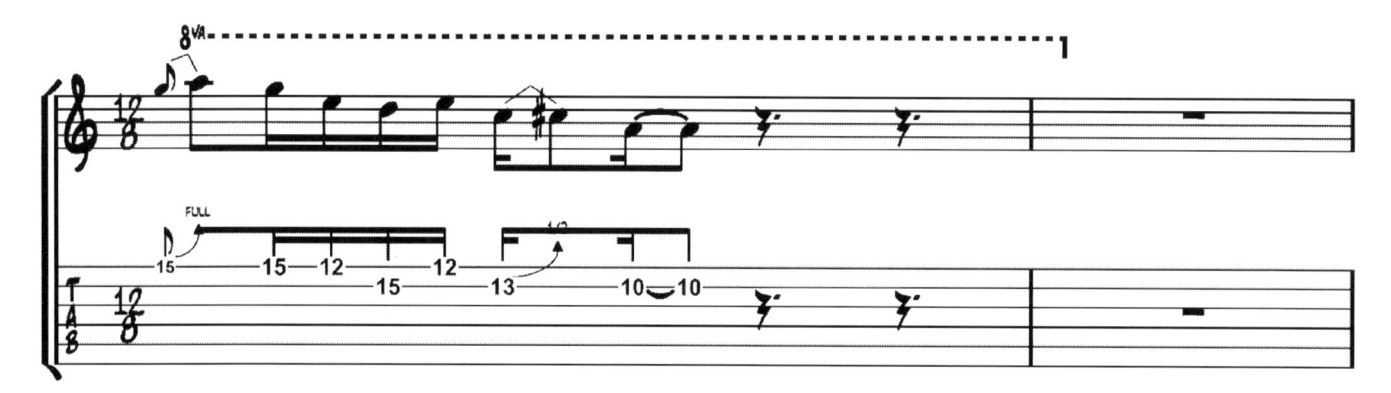

Example 5o:

We're starting to reach the upper range of the guitar when we use shape four in the key of A. Try using this shape in different positions on the fretboard in order to hear what these licks sound like in different keys.

Here are some ways to position shift from shape three into shape four using slides.

Example 5p (a):

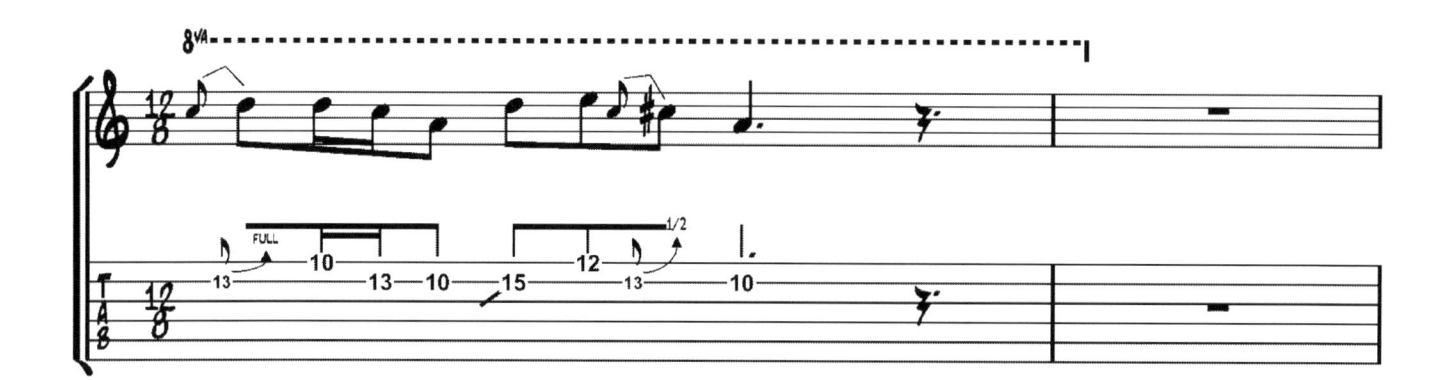

Example 5p (b):

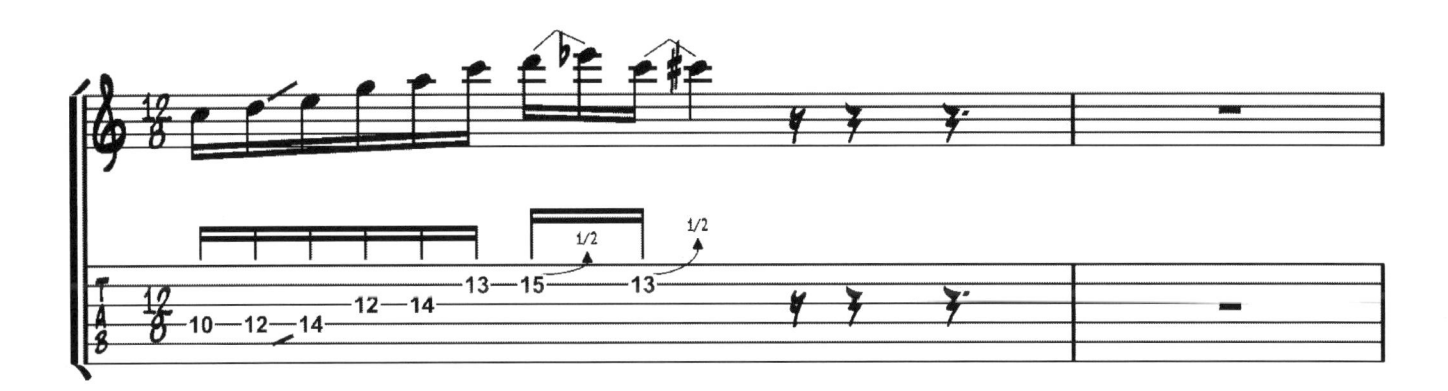

Example 5p (c):

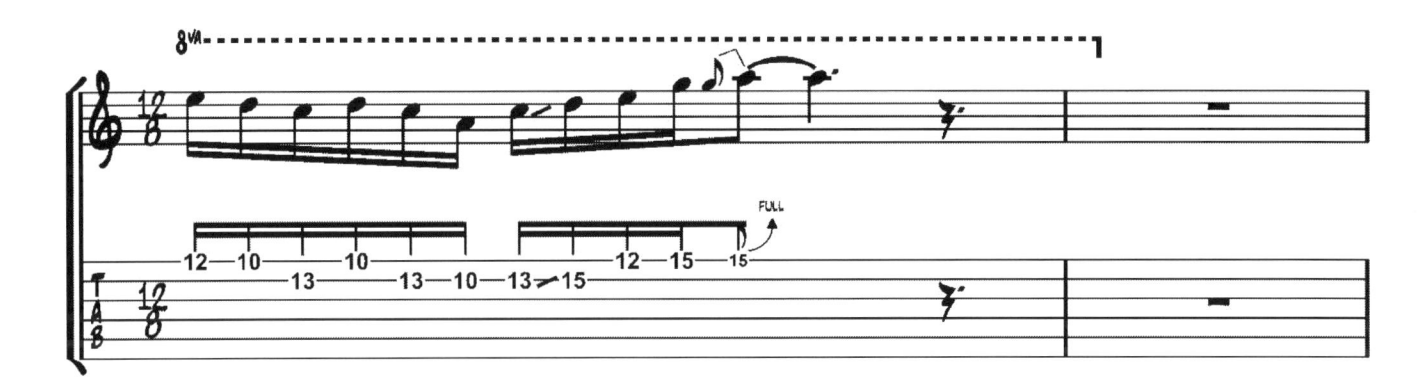

Shape four is my favourite scale shape to use when soloing. There is a lot of milage to be had here, so try soloing with it exclusively for a week: you'll be amazed how many 'standard' blues licks it contains.

A Minor Pentatonic Shape Five

Shape five is an interesting position. In my opinion it can be a little harder to use because the best notes to bend tend to fall on weak fingers. On the flip side, there are good opportunities for some big tone-and-a-half bends so with a little perseverance you should be able to get some useful results. One common thing to do with this shape is to *slide down into* shape five *from* shape one in order to add some bass notes below the root.

As we are reaching the top of the guitar now I have written the scale out in both the lower and higher octaves. Learn to use the scale in both positions and transpose it to other keys.

Example 5q (a):

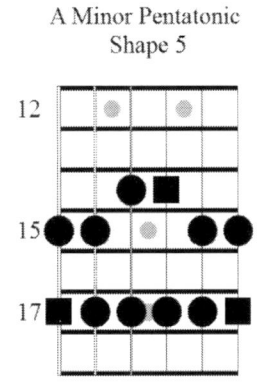

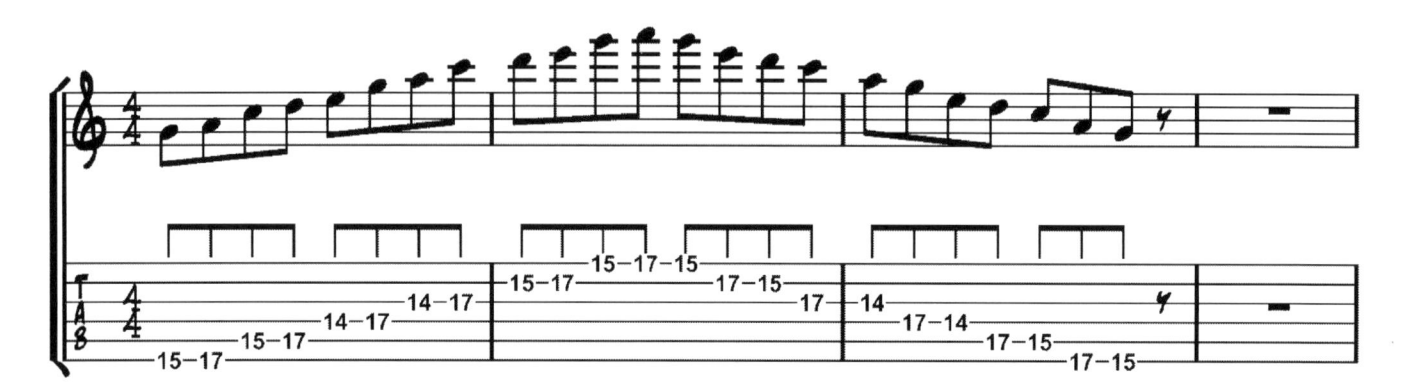

Example 5q (b):

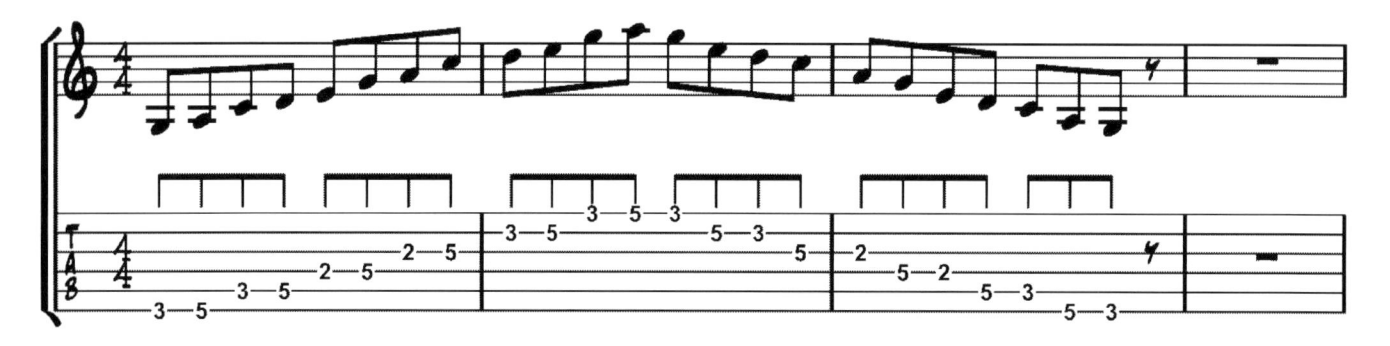

Once again, here are a few 'shortcut' licks to help you find some useful applications of this scale shape.

Example 5r:

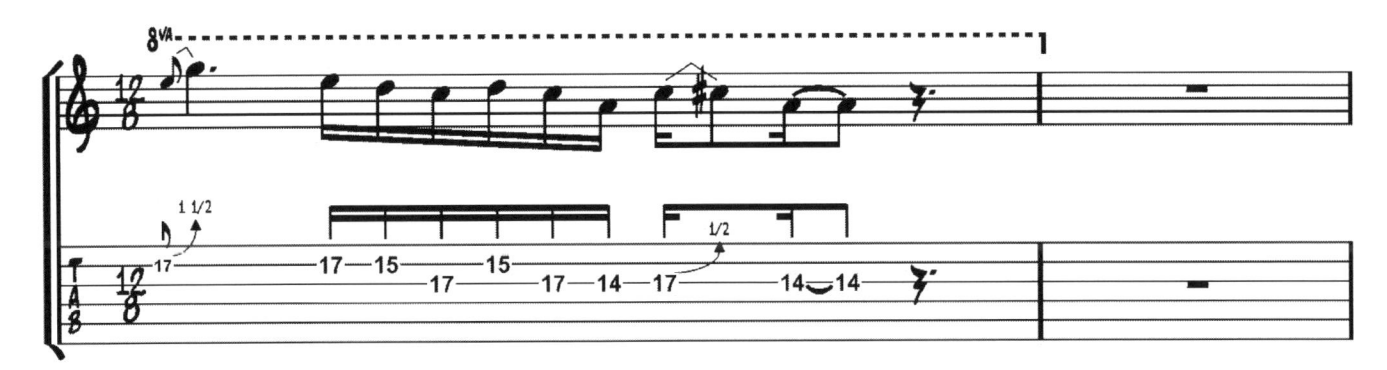

Example 5s:

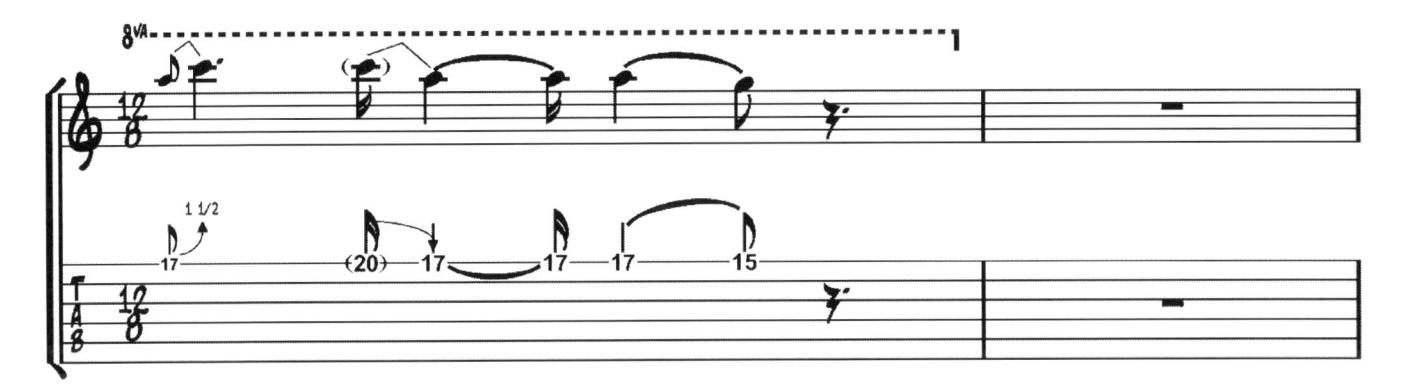

Example 5t:

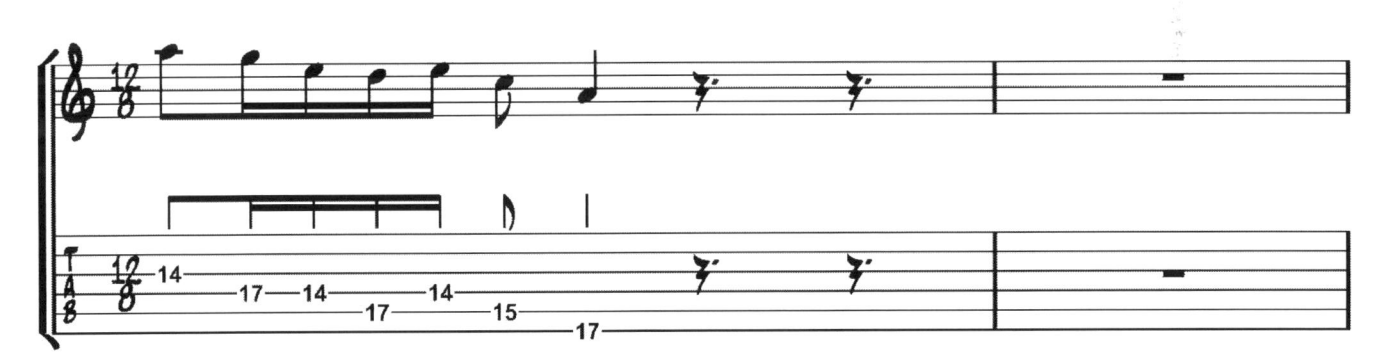

The following licks show a few methods of moving from shape four into shape five:

Example 5u (a):

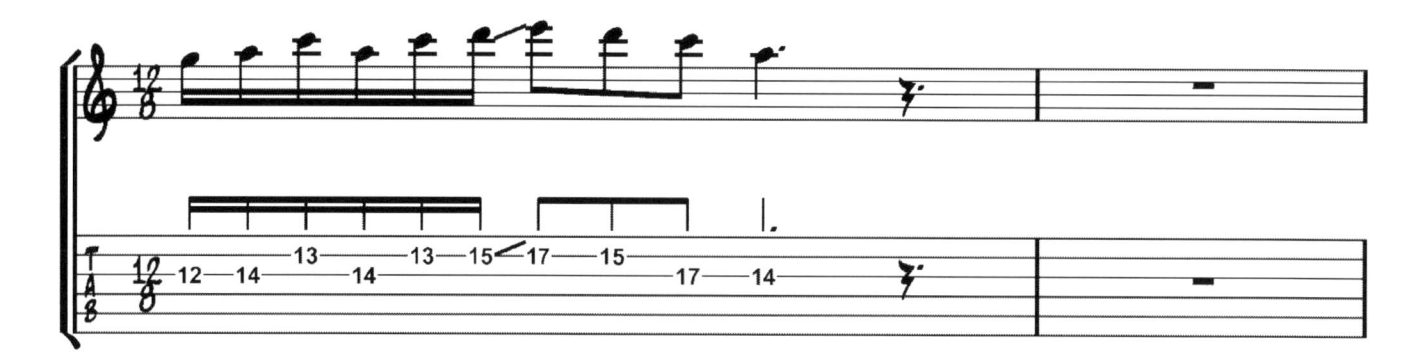

Example 5u (b):

Example 5u (c):

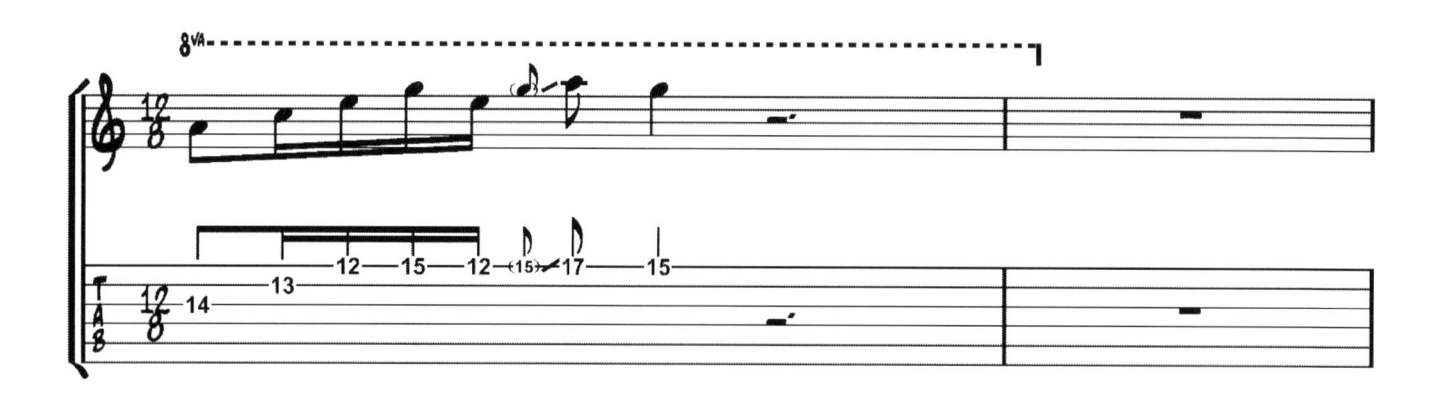

Linking Minor Pentatonic Shapes

Now we have looked at specific vocabulary and ideas for each of the five minor pentatonic shapes, we can look at some common ideas to link them together; from the bottom of the guitar neck to the top.

As ever, these are just a few possibilities so spend some of your practice time seeing how many ways you can find to move between all the different shapes on the guitar.

Example 5v:

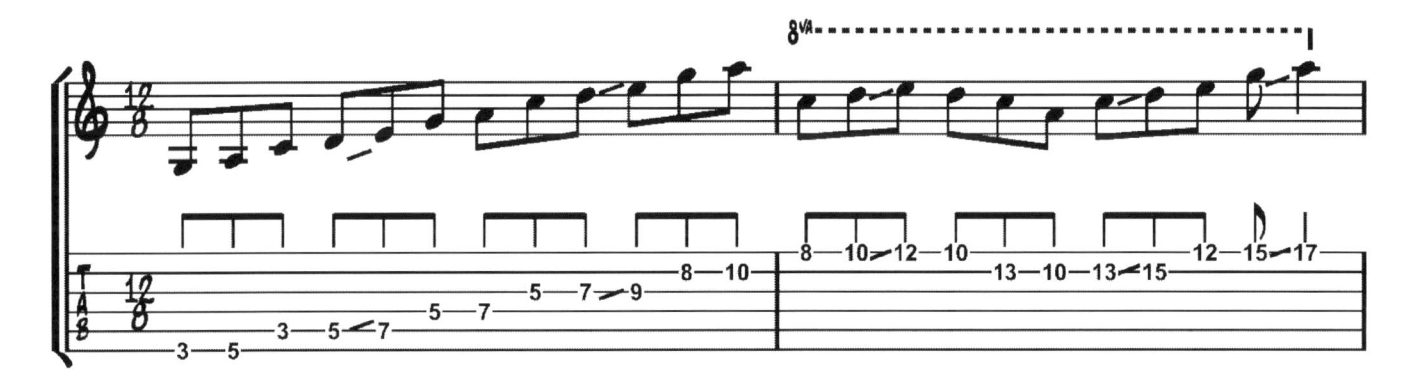

Example 5w:

Example 5x:

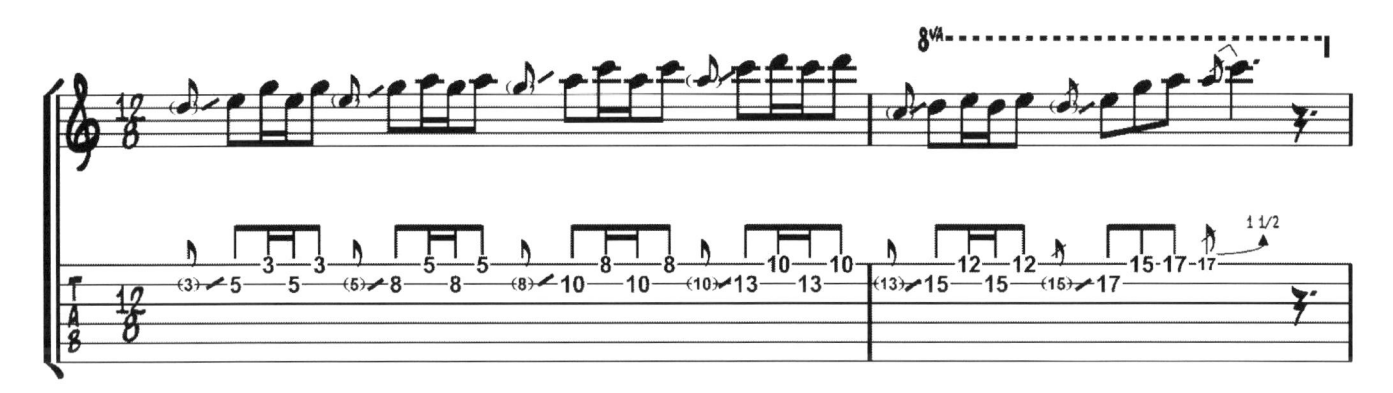

Conclusions

The Complete Guide to Blues Guitar Book Two deliberately set out *not* to be a 'lick book'. Even though there are hundreds of examples of blues vocabulary on these pages, they are all formed as a result of experimenting with, and demonstrating specific rhythmic, melodic and phrasing techniques.

I have tried to teach you the skills you need to transcend the need for licks, so that when you solo you are able to play the lines that you conceptualise and *feel* inside your head. This kind of control is what people are talking about when they say 'the music flows through them': There is no barrier between the music in their minds and what they can actually play on their instruments.

This level of freedom on your instrument is difficult to attain, but it's one of the most worthwhile pursuits in music. To have a melody appear in your head and to immediately be able to play it as you hear it is an incredible feeling.

This kind of expression is also a circular process: the more you study rhythm and phrasing (and of course scale choice and hitting chord changes - this will be covered in book three), the more your ears will awaken to thousands of new melodic possibilities. In most languages, you can't add a word to your own vocabulary unless you have heard or read it somewhere before. Our advantage now is that focused practice of rhythm, phrasing and creativity will *help you invent your own words*.

In this book I have given you the tools to create your own dialect within the established language of the blues. If you work on just one concept for long enough you will always come up with a new and personal way to play it. When you have studied three or four ideas they will start to combine and generate many exponential new possibilities.

Please don't think that I'm discounting learning licks, I'm not at all. To improve our writing skills and vocabulary we read the works of others and the same applies in music. The quickest way to sound like Jimi Hendrix is to transcribe and learn Jimi Hendrix's music. All I'm suggesting is that if we choose to learn his ideas, we should make them our own through the use of personal interpretation and phrasing.

I really hope that you have enjoyed this book and see it as a fresh approach to melodic soloing. The ideas contained here don't just apply to the blues; they are applicable to any form of music. Please take them and run with them.

Joseph

www.fundamental-changes.com

Don't forget the appendix in the back of this book to help you develop your vibrato and bending techniques.

If you like this book, please review it on Amazon

Appendix A Bending in Tune

The following exercises are all taken from my book **Complete Technique for Modern Guitar**

Bending

Bending notes with perfect intonation is probably the skill that really sets the professionals apart from amateurs. Other than good rhythm, perfect intonation is the main priority I give my students when they start playing rock guitar, because nothing ruins a solo more than an out-of-tune bend.

Once again, it is vital that we learn to bend accurately with each finger, and your 2nd, 3rd and 4th fingers should be capable of executing up to a *one-and-a-half tone* bend.

To bend a note on the guitar you should always support the bending finger with any spare fingers below it. In other words, if you are bending a note on the 3rd string, 7th fret with your 3rd finger, your 2nd finger (if not also your 1st) should also be on the string to give strength and control.

The idea behind all the exercises in this chapter is to play a reference note, descend the string a few frets and then bend perfectly back up to the reference. Treat this as an aural exercise; you are listening for the bent note to sound exactly like the reference pitch.

Try the following three exercises with different fingers on each bend. Go through each line 4 times, the first time bend with your 1st finger, then your 2nd etc. When you are on line three, don't worry about bending with your 1st finger.

Example 6a:

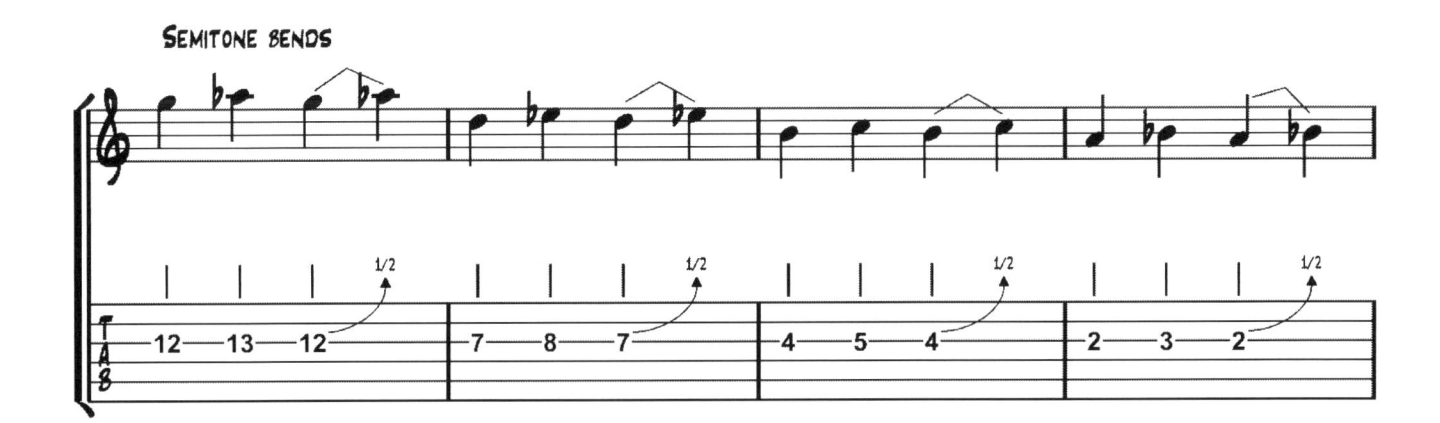

Example 6b:

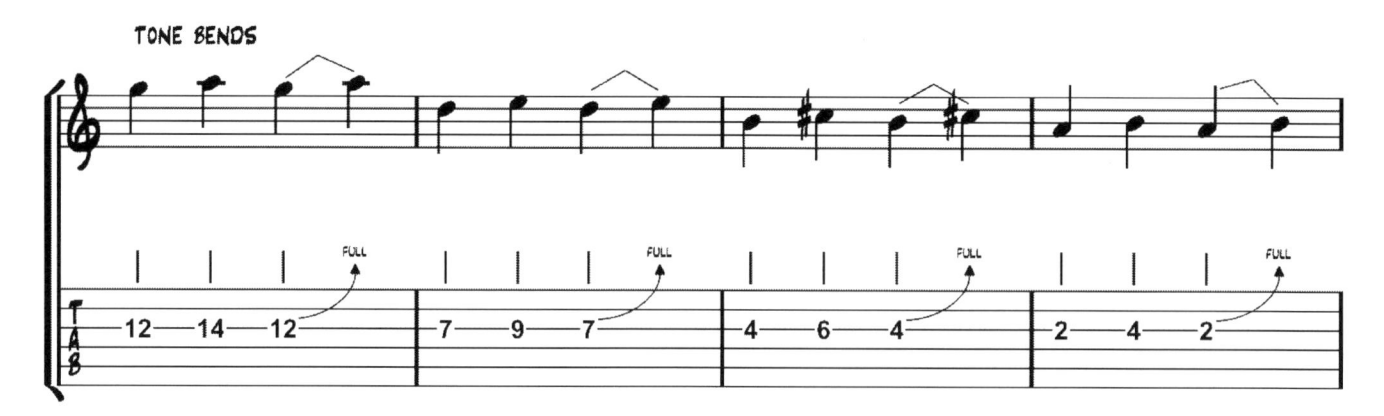

Example 6c:

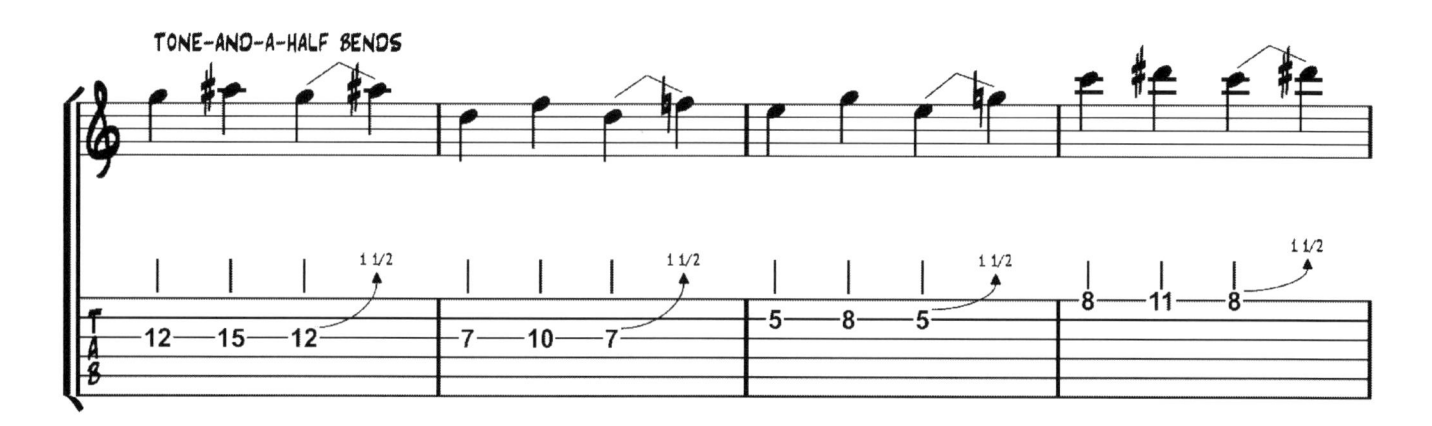

Begin the exercises by bending very slowly to pitch, this will give you time to *hear* if you are in tune. It also develops control and strength in the fretting hand fingers.

Gradually speed up the rate at which you bend to the target note. If you can hit it perfectly with an immediate, fast bend you know you have it.

Pre-bends

A pre-bend is essentially a bend in reverse. You bend the note to the desired pitch before picking it and releasing the bend. Pre-bends are notated like this:

Example 6d:

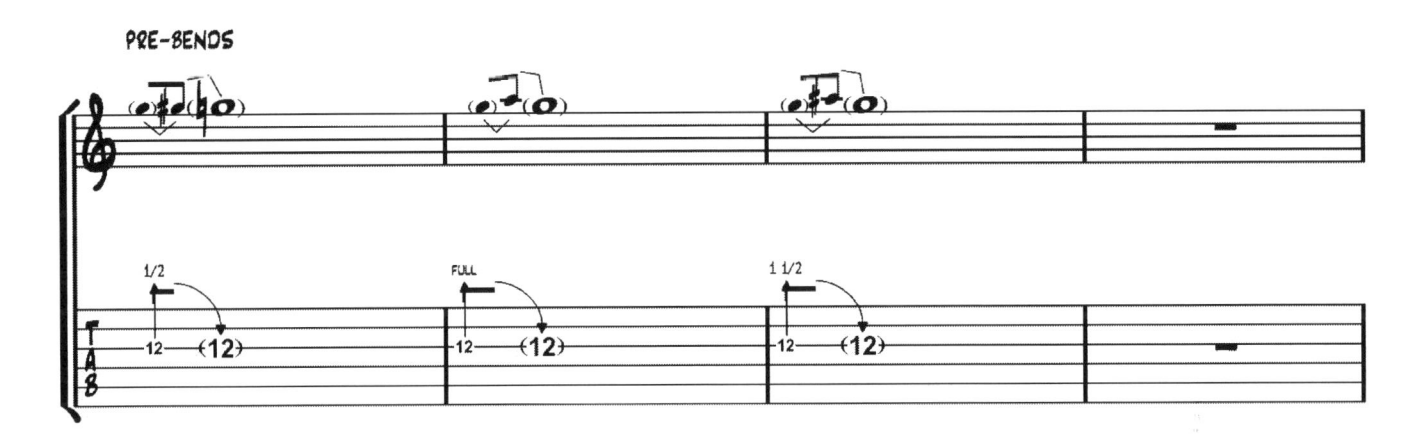

To practice this extremely expressive technique, go back through exercises 6a – c and modify them to include pre-bends in the following way:

Example 6e:

Do this with all fingers over all bend distances.

Unison Bends

Unison bends are when you play two notes together on adjacent strings. The higher note is normally not bent, while the lower note is bent up to sound identical to the higher one. Jimi Hendrix and Jimmy Page both made great use of this technique.

These bends are quite difficult to execute on a Floyd Rose tremolo and will always be slightly out of tune due to the nature of the mechanism, but with a bit of vibrato, intonation errors can be covered slightly.

A unison bend is notated in this way:

Example 6f:

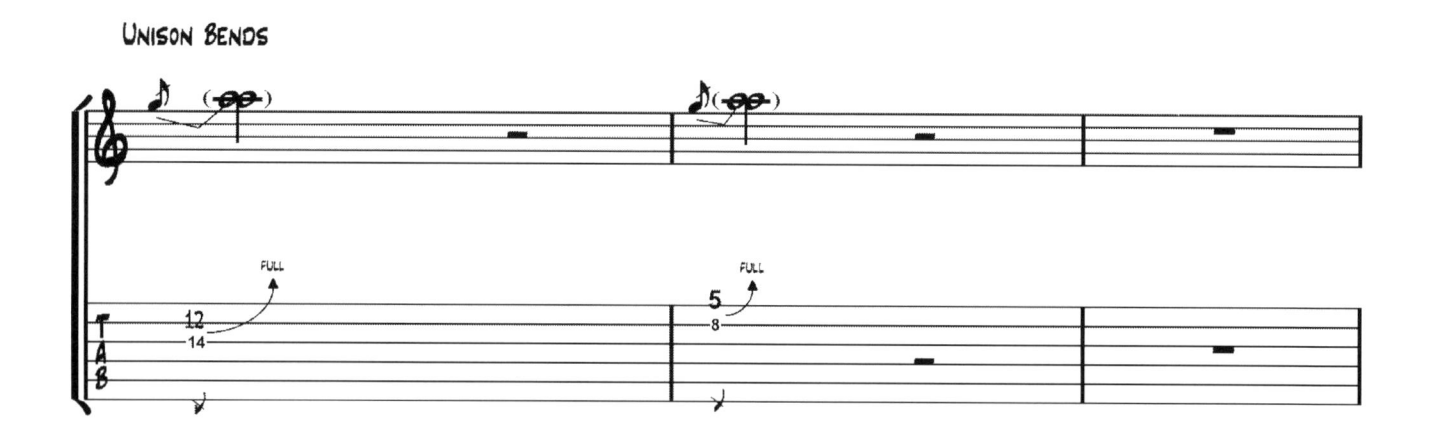

Try the following exercises to develop your control and accuracy:

Example 6g:

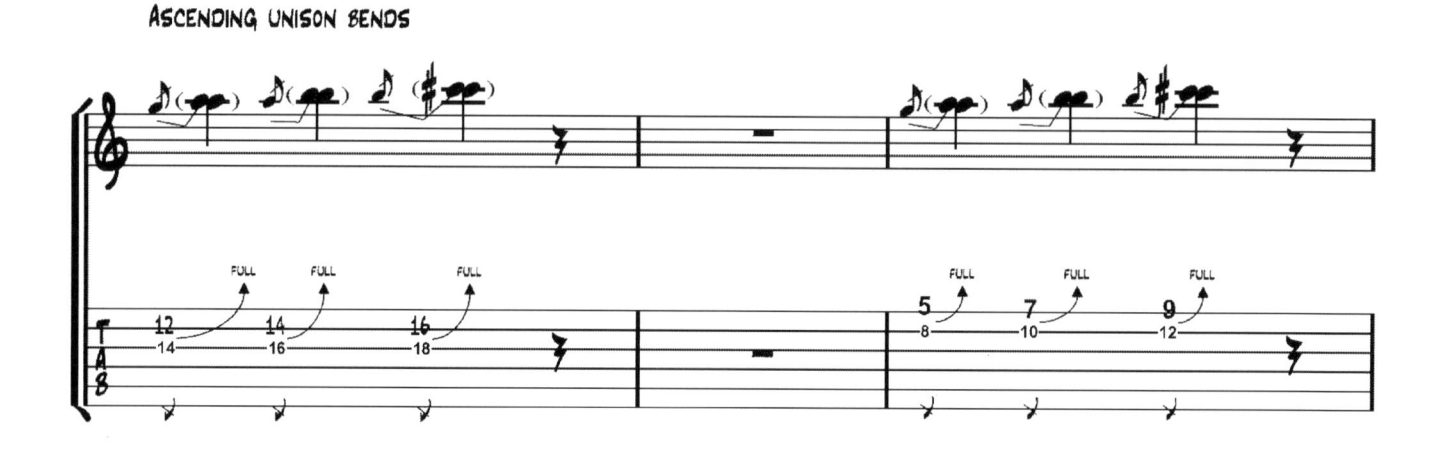

Double Stop Bends

A double stop is simply the act of playing two notes at the same time. A double stop bend is when you bend both notes. This is a very common technique in blues and rock guitar playing.

To execute a double stop bend, lay your finger flat, as described in the vibrato section, with your fingernail pointing towards you. However, this time, barre your finger across two adjacent strings. To bend the notes, rotate your wrist in the same manner as vibrato, but only do it once, slowly as you pick both strings. This is shown in the following exercise:

Example 6h:

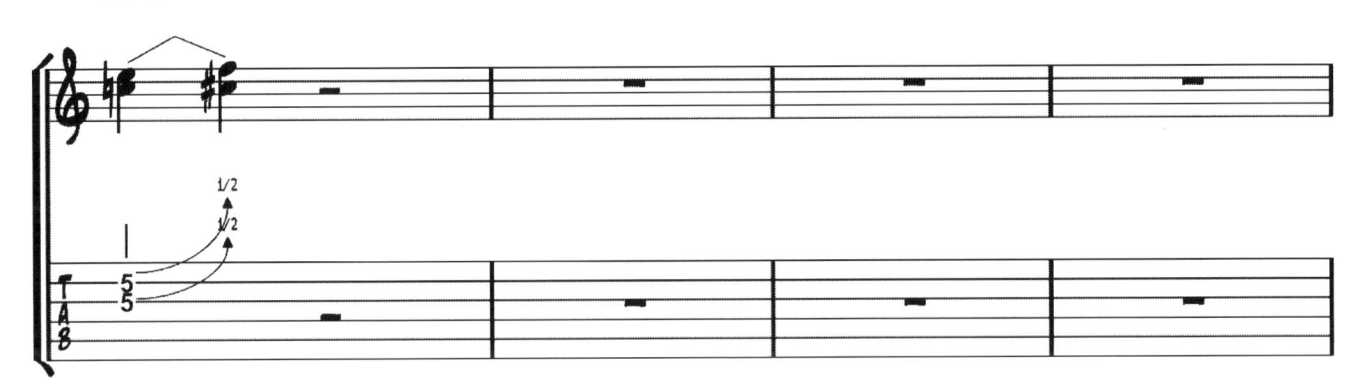

Try these all over the neck.

Appendix B Vibrato

In my opinion, vibrato is one of the two most important expressive effects. It gives your phrases a vocal quality and makes your music sing. There are many types, but here we will focus on just two, *axial* and *radial*.

Axial vibrato is when you quickly and repeatedly pull the string slightly sharp, *parallel* to the guitar string.

Radial vibrato is more similar to string bending; your wrist moves in a direction perpendicular to the guitar string, using a finger as a pivot on the underside of the neck. This is more difficult, but it does give extremely worthwhile results.

Axial Vibrato

To create axial vibrato, you simply press firmly on a fretted note and, making sure your wrist is soft, move your wrist quickly backwards and forwards parallel to the neck of the guitar. Often, your thumb will quickly release from the back of the neck to help with the speed of the wrist movement. This movement, combined with the pressure you place with your fingertip repeatedly pulls the string slightly sharp before releasing. This is an easy technique to give life and dynamics to your music whenever there is a longer, sustained note.
This is a subtle effect, and it is important to practice it with every finger of the fretting hand. It is actually much harder to produce good vibrato with the 4th finger than the first.

Here is an exercise to develop good axial vibrato:

Example 6i:

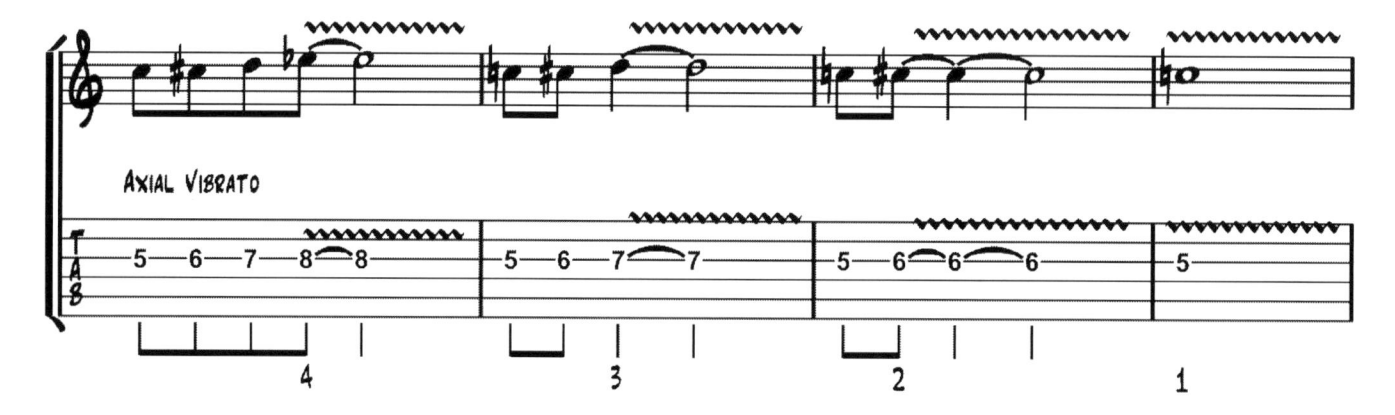

Remember to try removing your thumb from the back of the guitar neck to allow your wrist to move quickly and evenly backwards and forwards.

Also, practice moving between slow to fast and back to slow vibrato for added effect. Try the above example in different areas of the guitar neck and on different strings. They all feel different and require different types of control.

Add this kind of vibrato to any musical phrases or licks that you know. Take into account the tempo and groove of the song; you might want to sync your vibrato into 1/8th, 1/16th or 1/32 notes.

Radial Vibrato

Radial vibrato is a more difficult technique; it creates *much* wider vibrato which can often be up to a tone wide. Some guitarists go as far as to add vibrato which is a tone and a half wide when playing hard rock and fusion.

With radial vibrato we must greatly alter the position of the hand on the guitar neck so that we can *bend* the desired note up and down quickly. This involves using the *outside* part of the finger on the string, (so that your fingernail points straight down the neck towards you), and using the first finger as a lever or *pivot* against the underside of the neck to aid quick, repeated bends.

If you imagine turning a door knob, or the Queen of England waving, you will get the idea.

Radial vibrato is an individual technique which tends to be unique to each guitarist; however I will describe the method by which I get the best results. You may want to alter the following steps which apply to vibrato on the *1st* finger as you see fit. The ultimate goal is to achieve the ability to execute *tone wide* vibrato with *each* finger of the fretting hand.

1) Play and hold the desired note. Try playing the 7th fret on the 3rd string, with your 1st finger.
2) Roll your wrist *away* from you, so instead of playing the note with the tip of the 1st finger you are playing on its side. Pushing your elbow out away from you will help with this.
3) The nail of your first finger should now be pointing straight down the string towards you.
4) Push your 1st finger up, into the underside of the neck. It should connect with the neck just below the knuckle on the first of your three finger sections (closest to your palm).
5) Let your thumb creep over the top of the neck and relax your wrist, so your unused fingers fall and fan out slightly.
6) Using your already-placed 1st finger as a pivot, turn your wrist *away* from you to bend the string down towards the floor, pulling it slightly sharp.
7) Relax the pressure in your wrist and hand to let the string release back to its starting position.
8) Repeat this as many times as you can.

At first you won't move the string very far and it may become sore on the side of your finger quite quickly. When this happens take a break.

As you get stronger and your skin becomes tougher, you will be able to move the string further and more quickly. The key to all this, is to always use the *side* of the finger, and always have a pivoting finger under the neck.

I like to build redundancy into my playing, so I spend time practicing bending the string much further than I would ever realistically use. If you can work your way up to a tone-and-a-half vibrato then you're doing very well. In my playing I normally use a semi-tone.
The following exercises will help you develop vibrato strength, depth and speed on all fingers.

Example 6j:

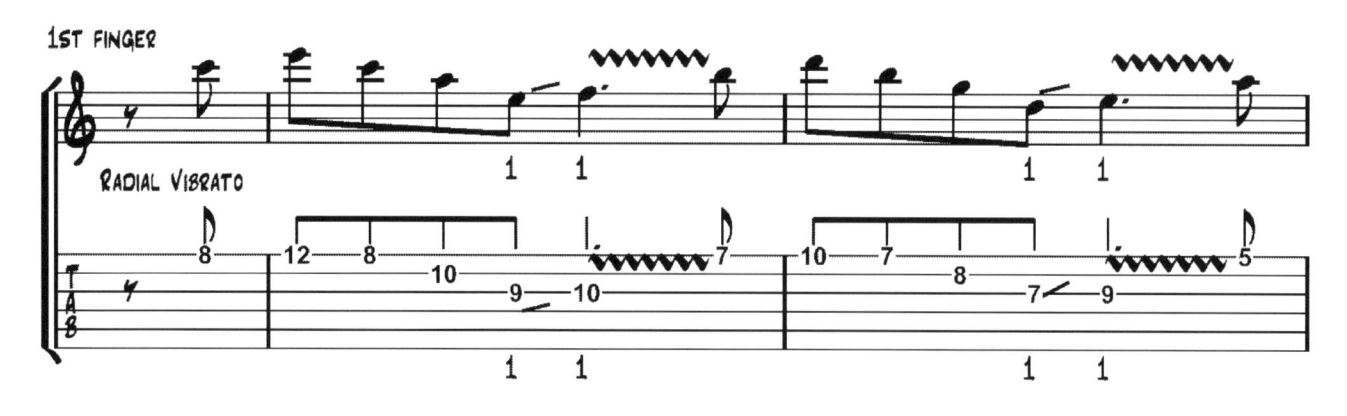

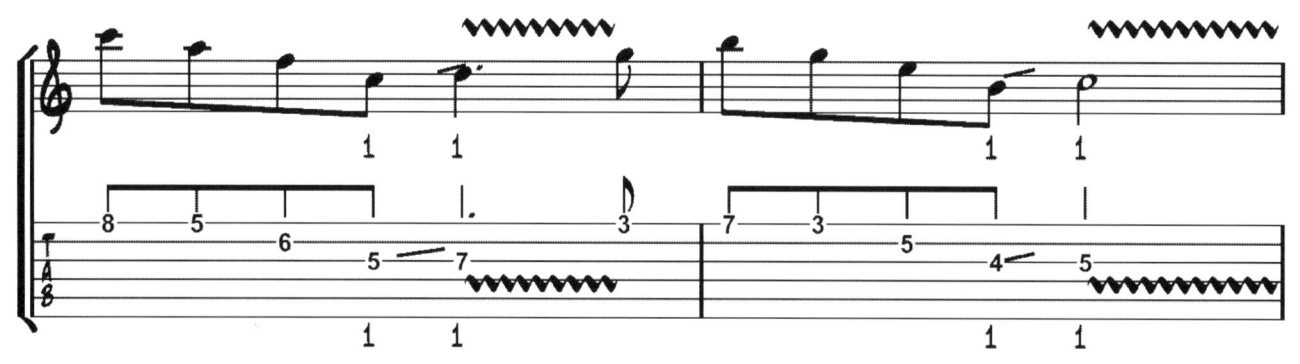

Example 6k:

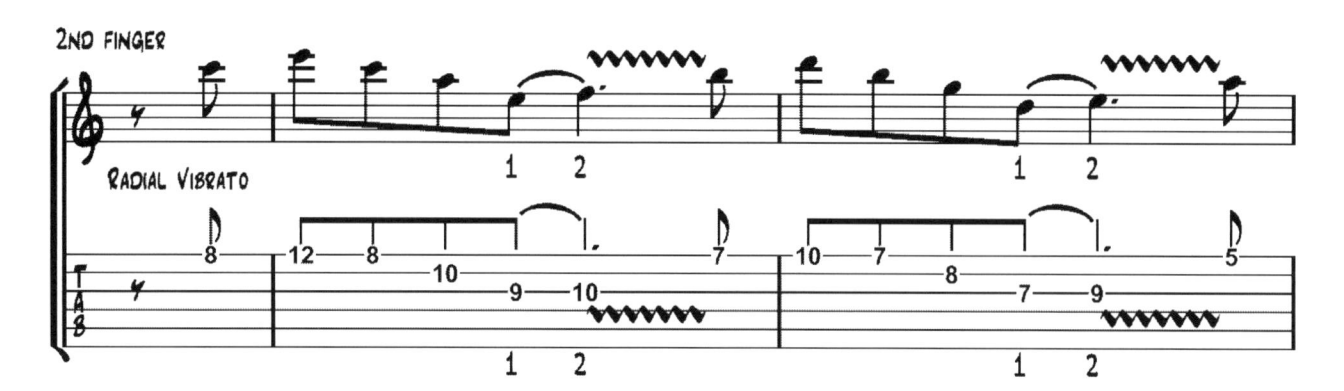

Example 6l:

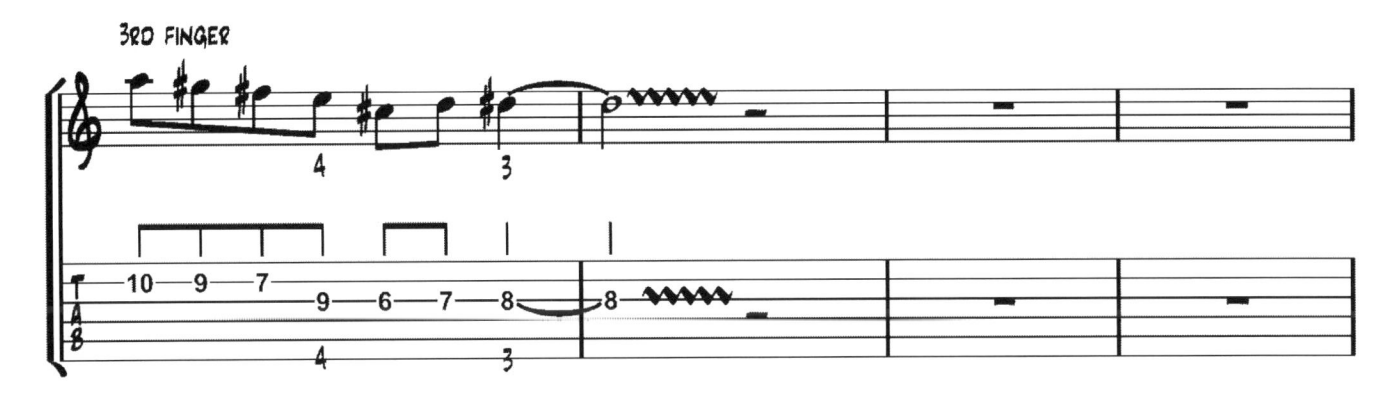

Example 6m:

* It is difficult and unusual to place the 4th finger on its side in the same manner as the other fingers. You should still roll it slightly, but use your other fingers placed on the string behind it to add strength and support.

Vibrato is a difficult technique that may take longer to develop than the other skills in this book. Try to spend 5 minutes every day working on your depth, speed and coordination with each finger.

Try the ideas in this section over different string groupings, and in different positions on the guitar.

Vibrato is much more difficult towards the lower frets.

Other Books from Fundamental Changes

The Complete Guide to Playing Blues Guitar Book One: Rhythm Guitar

The Complete Guide to Playing Blues Guitar Book Three: Beyond Pentatonics

The Complete Guide to playing Blues Guitar Compilation

The CAGED System and 100 Licks for Blues Guitar

Fundamental Changes in Jazz Guitar: The Major ii V I

Minor ii V Mastery for Jazz Guitar

Jazz Blues Soloing for Guitar

Guitar Scales in Context

Guitar Chords in Context Part One

Jazz Guitar Chord Mastery (Guitar Chords in Context Part Two)

Complete Technique for Modern Guitar

The Complete Technique, Theory and Scales Compilation for Guitar

Sight Reading Mastery for Guitar

Rock Guitar Un-CAGED: The CAGED System and 100 Licks for Rock Guitar

The Practical Guide to Modern Music Theory for Guitarists

Beginner's Guitar: The Essential Guide

All Audio files in this book are available from www.fundamental-changes.com/audio-downloads

Be Social

Join over 4000 people getting six free guitar lessons each day on Facebook:

www.facebook.com/FundamentalChangesInGuitar

Keep up to date on Twitter: @Guitar_Joseph

Cover Photo © Can Stock Photo Inc. / johnraffaghello

Made in the USA
Middletown, DE
20 June 2017